The Big Book of
Picture-Book
Authors & Illustrators

by James Preller

S C H O L A S T I C
PROFESSIONAL BOOKS

New York • Toronto • London • Auckland • Sydney
Mexico City • New Delhi • Hong Kong • Buenos Aires

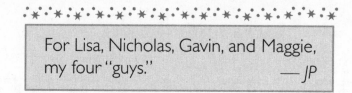

For Lisa, Nicholas, Gavin, and Maggie,
my four "guys."
— JP

Grateful acknowledgment is made to the following authors, publishers, and other copyright holders for permission to reprint the following covers and photographs:

From AUNT HARRIET'S UNDERGROUND RAILROAD IN THE SKY by Faith Ringgold reprinted with permission of Random House Children's Books. Copyright © 1992 by Faith Ringgold.

From RECHENKA'S EGGS by Patricia Polacco, copyright © 1988 by Patricia Polacco. Used by permission of Philomel Books, an imprint of Penguin Putnam Books for Young Readers, a division of Penguin Putnam Inc.

From THE VERY HUNGRY CATERPILLAR by Eric Carle, copyright © 1969 and 1987 by Eric Carle. Used by permission of Philomel Books, an imprint of Penguin Putnam Books for Young Readers, a division of Penguin Putnam Inc.

Photos: Mitsumasa Anno: courtesy of Penguin Putnam; Tedd Arnold: courtesy of Penguin Putnam; Molly Bang: courtesy of Scholastic Inc.; Shonto Begay: Nancy Dahl; Aliki Brandenberg: courtesy of HarperCollins, Val Lambros; Jan Brett: courtesy of Putnam's Sons; Norman Bridwell: © 1988, courtesy of Michael Newler; Marc Brown: courtesy of Scholastic Inc., Walter Silver; Ashley Bryan: courtesy of Simon & Schuster, Matthew Wysocki; Eric Carle: courtesy of Penguin, © S. Petegorsky; Barbara Cooney: courtesy of Penguin Putnam; Donald Crews: courtesy of Nina Crews; Lulu Delacre: Cynthia DelCart; Tomie dePaola: courtesy of Penguin Putnam, Suki Coughlin; Diane and Leo Dillon: courtesy of Scholastic Inc.; Lois Ehlert: courtesy of Harcourt, Lillian Schultz; Mem Fox: courtesy of Harcourt, Randy Larcombe; Gail Gibbons: courtesy of HarperCollins; Patricia Reilly Giff: courtesy of Bantam Doubleday Dell Books, Tornberg Associates; Phoebe Gilman: courtesy of Scholastic Canada; Paul Goble: courtesy of Simon & Schuster, Janet Goble; Eloise Greenfield: courtesy of Scholastic Inc.; Ruth Heller: courtesy of Penguin Putnam; Kevin Henkes: courtesy of HarperCollins, Tom Beckley; Gloria Houston: courtesy of HarperCollins; Pat Hutchins: courtesy of Greenwillow Books, © Photocraft (Hampstead) Ltd.; Trina Schart Hyman: Bernie Goedhardt; Tony Johnston: courtesy of HarperCollins; Ezra Jack Keats: courtesy of Penguin Putman; Steven Kellogg: courtesy of Dial; Karla Kuskin: courtesy of HarperCollins, Piper Productions; Leo Lionni: courtesy of Houghton Mifflin; Arnold Lobel: courtesy of HarperCollins, Van Williams; Jonathan London: Bhakti Smith; James Marshall: courtesy of Penguin Books; Bill Martin, Jr.: courtesy of Henry Holt, Sigrid Estrada; Jean Marzollo: courtesy of HarperCollins, Ellen Warner; Robert McCloskey: courtesy of Penguin USA, Mary Velthoven; Emily Arnold McCully: courtesy of Putnam; Angela Shelf Medearis: courtesy of Scholastic Inc.; Robert Munsch: courtesy of Scholastic Canada; Mary Pope Osborne: courtesy of Random House Children's Books, Paul Coughlin; Barbara Park: courtesy of Random House Children's Books; Dav Pilkey: courtesy of Scholastic Inc.; Jerry Pinkney: courtesy of Penguin Putnam, © Myles Pinkney; J. Brian Pinkney: courtesy of Random House Children's Books; Patricia Polacco: courtesy of Penguin Putnam, © Kenn Klein; Jack Prelutsky: courtesy of Random House Children's Books; Barbara Reid: courtesy of Scholastic Inc.; Faith Ringgold: courtesy of Bernice Gallery Steinbaum, C. Love; Joanne Ryder: courtesy of Simon & Schuster, Deborah Jaffe; Cynthia Rylant: courtesy of Simon & Schuster; Allen Say: courtesy of Houghton Mifflin; Jon Scieszka: courtesy of Penguin Putnam, Brian Smale ; Maurice Sendak: courtesy of HarperCollins, Chris Callis; Dr. Seuss: courtesy of Random House; Peter Sis: courtesy of Farrar, Strauss & Giroux, © Palma Fiacco Fotografin; Lane Smith: David Godlis; Peter Spier: courtesy of Doubleday, David Osika; William Steig: © Nancy Crampton; John Steptoe: courtesy of HarperCollins; Mark Teague: courtesy of Scholastic Inc.; Chris Van Allsburg: courtesy of Houghton Mifflin; Bernard Waber: courtesy of Houghton Mifflin; Kate Waters: courtesy of Scholastic Photo Resources; Rosemary Wells: courtesy of Penguin Putnam, © Nelvana Productions; Hans Wilhelm: courtesy of Scholastic Inc.; Vera B. Williams: courtesy of HarperCollins, © Susan Kuklin; Jane Yolen: courtesy of Simon & Schuster; Ed Young: courtesy of Harcourt, Sean Kernan; Charlotte Zolotow: courtesy of de Grummond Children's Literature Collections, University of Southern Mississippi; James Preller: Lisa Preller

Cover design Norma Ortiz
Interior design by Sydney Wright (based on a design by Solutions by Design, Inc.)
Photo research by Jessica Moon and Sarah Longacre

ISBN: 0-439-20154-3
Copyright © 2001 by James Preller.
All rights reserved. Printed in the U.S.A.

Contents

Picture-Book Authors & Illustrators

Introduction

Welcome to *The Big Book of Picture-Book Authors and Illustrators*! This all-in-one resource is a great way to introduce children to 75 of their favorite authors and illustrators, including Aliki, Eric Carle, Tomie dePaola, Kevin Henkes, Leo Lionni, Jerry Pinkney, Patricia Polacco, Dr. Seuss, and many more. The interview-based profiles in this collection provide insight into the lives, work, inspiration, and creative process of these talented writers and artists. Share these fascinating mini-biographies with students to enhance author studies and help your students read with greater enthusiasm and understanding.

Great effort went into selecting the authors and illustrators included in this book. We spoke with a number of teachers and school librarians to find out which authors and illustrators students would most like to read about. James Preller spent many illuminating hours conducting the interviews and gathering information before writing the profiles that appear on these pages.

Each of these creative people offers his or her distinct voice and vision. Some make us chuckle, others make us cry, some rely on facts to tell of dramatic events that shaped our history, others spin yarns in irresistible verse. These authors and illustrators bring a rich diversity of experience to their work. They come from near and far: big cities and small towns all over the United States, as well as Puerto Rico, Australia, Canada, Czechoslovakia, China, England, Germany, Holland, Japan, and Northern Ireland.

And they all have great stories to tell. Faith Ringgold reflects on a wonderful childhood in Harlem; Shonto Begay explains what it's like growing up in a hogan on a Navajo reservation; Cynthia Rylant describes the influence of her Appalachian upbringing on her work; and Mem Fox shares the thrill of publishing her first book—after rewriting it 23 times!

Each profile is accompanied by a "Do It Yourself" activity—in most cases, suggested by the authors and illustrators themselves—to spark students' creativity to tell their own stories. We suggest that you adapt these activities to meet the needs of your students. For example, younger children might draw pictures and dictate stories while older children might work through the writing process to create polished stories for their portfolios.

We designed this book with your students in mind. By learning about their favorite authors and illustrators, children gain valuable insight into the stories they are reading. This encourages children to read and provides them with models of strong writing, ultimately helping them develop into more fluent, capable, and motivated readers and writers.

Our hope is that this collection of interviews will help you and your students feel even more connected to these wonderfully creative authors and illustrators. And who knows . . . it may just inspire your students to publish their own books someday.

—*The Editors*

Preface

Writing this book has given me the chance to meet some of the great authors and illustrators in children's literature. I asked questions, discussed the creative process, listened to their stories, and learned—not because I was such an astute student, but because the information was so good. How could I walk away from a conversation with Faith Ringgold without feeling uplifted in some way, and grateful, literally *gifted* by the experience: I got to talk to Faith Ringgold!

Lucky me.

When it came time to write the actual profiles of each artist, I kept telling myself one thing: Get out of the way, Jimmy! That is: Trust the material. So I've tried to step away and allow these talented, creative individuals to step forward . . . and speak.

May this book, like any good turn, lead you to another.

—James Preller

Picture-Book
Authors & Illustrators

Mitsumasa Anno

Born: March 20, 1926, in Tsuwano, Japan
Home: Tokyo, Japan

SELECTED TITLES

Topsy-Turvies: Pictures to Stretch the Imagination
1970

Anno's Alphabet: An Adventure in Imagination
1974

Anno's Journey
1977

The King's Flower
1979

Anno's Medieval World
1980

Anno's U.S.A.
1983

All in a Day
1986

Anno's Math Games (first in a series)
1987

Anno's Aesop: A Book of Fables by Aesop and Mr. Fox
1989

Anno's Magic Seeds
1995

Mitsumasa Anno was born and raised in Tsuwano, a small mountain village in Japan. Though it was a very beautiful village surrounded by mountains, Anno yearned to learn more about the world beyond it. Anno remembers, "As a child, I always wondered what was on the other side of the mountains."

Anno's boundless curiosity pertained not only to distant lands; he was also fascinated by mathematics, logic, entomology (the study of insects), and art. He possessed a lively imagination: "I liked to observe real people and make up stories about them. If a man walked by, I would think that he must be a carpenter or a doctor on his way to see a child in the hospital or whatever."

In 1961 Anno first saw the drawings of M.C. Escher. These strange, improbable drawings excited Anno. It seemed to him that Escher's drawings were almost like puzzles, riddles from another world—the world of the imagination. Newly inspired, Anno decided to create his own, Escher-like illustrations. In the book *Topsy-Turvies: Pictures to Stretch the Imagination*, he created impossible pictures of ceilings that double as floors, stairways that lead up to a lower level, and water faucets that turn into rivers.

Anno wanted the book to challenge readers to see new things and think new thoughts. In a postscript to the book he explained, "I have purposely added no words to these topsy-turvy pictures of mine so you can make them mean whatever you want them to mean."

Anno soon contrived another "book without rules"—*Upside-Downers: More Pictures to Stretch the Imagination*. He said, "My pictures are like maps, which perhaps only I can understand. Therefore, in following my maps there are some travelers who get

lost." But for Anno, getting lost is just one more opportunity for the reader to find something new.

"It seems that although languages and customs are different in various parts of the world, there are no differences at all in our hearts."

Anno's Journeys

Anno's first visit to Europe inspired him to write *Anno's Journey.* Anno said of his journey, "My purpose for traveling was not merely to see more of the world but to get lost in it. I did often get lost and faced many difficulties, but under such circumstances there were always unexpected discoveries and interesting experiences waiting for me."

Anno's Journey was the first of four remarkable books based on Anno's travels; it was followed by *Anno's Italy, Anno's Britain,* and *Anno's U.S.A.* Perhaps the most surprising thing that Anno discovered in his travels was how similar people are to one another. He says, "Among living creatures, more things are shared than are different. Seeing a sunset in Europe, I was impressed by the natural truth that we have only one sun—that no matter where we are, we all see the same sun." Differences such as language, dress, and skin color are only on the surface. As Anno said, "The essence of being human is the same everywhere."

Over time, many authors become associated with a particular character they created. For example, Dr. Seuss will forever be known as the man behind the Cat in the Hat, Norman Bridwell is beloved for Clifford the Big Red Dog, and H.A. Rey is famous for creating the mischievous Curious George. But Anno's books rarely center on a main character. Instead, they seem to be about the world itself. Still, there is one recurring character—the lone horseman who travels through the pages of the Journey series. This character best represents the spirit of Anno's work— the spirit of exploration and discovery.

The Journey books also provide readers with a treasure hunt of sorts. Hidden in the drawings are pictures of famous paintings or picture-book characters such as Goldilocks and Little Red Riding Hood. By hiding these treasures, Anno whispers a secret into the reader's ear: The more you seek, the more you shall find.

DO IT YOURSELF!

When he finished *Anno's Italy,* Anno said, "The book has no words, yet I feel sure that anyone who looks at it can understand what the people in the pictures are doing and what they are thinking and feeling." Do you think that's true? Try to imagine what some of the people in Anno's illustrations are thinking and feeling. Write down a conversation they might be having.

Tedd Arnold

Born: January 20, 1949, in Elmira, New York
Home: Elmira, New York

SELECTED TITLES

No Jumping on the Bed!
1987

The Signmaker's Assistant
1992

Green Wilma
1993

Five Ugly Monsters
1995

Inside a Barn in the Country
1995

*No More Water
in the Tub!*
1995

Huggly Gets Dressed
(first in a series)
1997

Parts
1997

Axle Annie
1999

Inside a Zoo in the City
2000

> *"I don't draw much before I write. Perhaps I will doodle with a few character sketches. But once I start writing and going through the editorial process, I don't draw at all."*

Tedd Arnold enjoys visiting classrooms. More to the point, he finds it *necessary.* Tedd explains, "Now that my kids are older, it's easy to forget what young children are like. Continuing to visit with kids is very important to me. I need to see what makes them laugh, what makes them tick. I don't want to lose track of their squirmy little reality."

Tedd hopes to leave children with a simple message: Reading is fun. "That's the reason I'm out there," Tedd says. "I want them to go away thinking that they can be writers and illustrators, too. It's something within the realm of their possibility. Hopefully some of them can take that to heart."

During his classroom visits, Tedd brings an easel to draw pictures for the audience. He talks about his work and answers questions. Tedd admits, "The number one question seems to be, 'Where do you get your ideas?' It's also the hardest question to answer because every idea is different. Some ideas seem to pop out of thin air—while I'm in the shower or walking my dog. Others come from reading or research. But most of my ideas come from my family and the things they do and say."

Tedd tells a wonderful story about the inspiration for the book *Parts.* "One time when my first son, Walter, was five years old, I found him lying on the couch, looking pale as a ghost . . . When I asked what was wrong, he wouldn't answer.

"In fact, he tried to talk to us without opening his mouth. It was really hard to understand him. Walter finally said there was something wrong with one of his teeth. That's when we figured out he had his first loose tooth! Walter

was scared to death because he thought he was falling apart!"

Tedd immediately recognized the humor—and the emotional truth—of the situation. Thinking it might be a good topic for a nonsense poem, Tedd jotted a few lines of verse in his journal. Then he promptly forgot all about it—for ten long years!

"I'm not sure what got me to pull that idea out," Tedd confesses. But for whatever reason, he returned to his journal and found that old verse. Tedd recalls, "It was about eight lines long. The key line in it, even then, was: *The glue that holds our parts together isn't holding me . . .*"

The basic idea sat and waited, untouched for ten years. Now it was ready. Or perhaps now *Tedd* was ready. Only this time he realized that the idea was not for a poem but rather a book!

The Artist Guy

Throughout his childhood Tedd's family moved often. By high school he'd already attended eight different schools. Tedd's artistic talent helped ease those transitions. "I was always drawing," Tedd recalls. "In school my cartoons graced many a desktop, chalkboard, and math paper. I could always get an identity as being The Artist Guy. I used my art as a way to find my niche in the new situations."

After college Tedd pursued his art by illustrating science textbooks and then by running his own graphic design studio. Meanwhile, Tedd became interested in children's books—largely through his wife, Carol, who was a kindergarten teacher. "She collected picture books," he explains. In time, Tedd became fascinated by the books, enjoying the playful way words and pictures worked together to form a whole. He recognized that it wasn't all that different from his work in advertising, where words (headlines and copy) and images come together to convey a message.

Tedd's apprenticeship in children's literature began: "Each evening after work I rushed to the library, brought home piles of children's books, and studied them cover to cover." Success did not come effortlessly—or instantly. His work was rejected for six years before finally being accepted. "If I heard feedback, I took it seriously and worked on it," Tedd says of those years. "I wasn't frustrated when they wouldn't accept my 'brilliant work.' I was willing to learn. I continued to adapt it. To study it. To try to see what it was they were looking for. And try to find that within me."

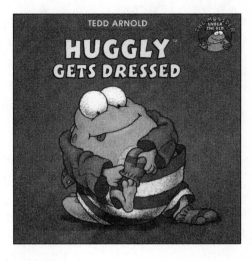

TEDD ARNOLD
HUGGLY GETS DRESSED

Molly Bang

Born: December 29, 1943, in Princeton, New Jersey
Home: Woods Hole, Massachusetts

Although making a picture book can be a long, painstaking process, Molly Bang genuinely seems to enjoy each step. Most important, she values the team effort that goes into making a book. Molly explains, "It's really a pleasure to work with editors and art directors who are trying to make this a good piece of work. At a certain point, you are working on this same thing that belongs to all of you. They want to make it better, and you want to make it better. Sometimes you just disagree on what's going to make it better."

Try and Try Again

Molly says, "With *The Paper Crane*, I did three versions of pictures before I did the published version. Each had a totally different style. One was Chinese brush painting; one was in pencil and white ink on gray paper, sort of like *Wiley and the Hairy Man*; the other used cut paper and featured one character that was an old woman. The editors rejected it because they thought she looked too weird. I thought she looked wonderful."

With each editorial rejection, Molly would shrug and say to herself, Oh well, try again. Finally, she hit upon a technique for the illustrations that everyone loved. "I used scissors, an X-acto blade, and construction paper," Bang recalls. "I picked up the pieces with tweezers, dipped them in glue, and attached them to the paper. It took about a year to make all the pictures."

Editors helped Molly in other ways too. Molly admits, "My tendency is to get too gushy and wordy. So my editors help me to revise and shorten the text." With *The Paper Crane*, her editors, Susan Hirschman and Libby Shub, suggested that the story might be improved if she included a child. Molly thought about the suggestion and agreed. She says, "I think that made it that much more interesting for me. Because then you've got two plots going on at once. The dad was just interested in running a great restaurant, but the child loved the bird and lost it."

> **"My mother can read Bengali, so she translated some folktales, which I then illustrated. There were never any problems; she was the boss of the words and I was the boss of the pictures."**

Molly points out that the boy isn't in the written story at all. "If you notice, the child is not in the words—he's just in the pictures." In this example, you can clearly see how a story is told not only in words but also in pictures. And sometimes a picture doesn't need any words to tell its story. If you need proof, just take a look at Molly's wordless book, *The Grey Lady and the Strawberry Snatcher*.

Most of Molly's books are the result of endless revisions, but there are some rare exceptions. Molly recalls, "I've never had a story that just came to me out of the blue, except for *Ten, Nine, Eight*, which came to me word for word. There it was; that was the only version. I didn't make a single change. What happened was, I was away from my daughter for a couple of weeks. I missed her and I wanted to write something for her. So *Ten, Nine, Eight* is what I wrote."

Molly Bang honed her writing skills by studying folktales. As she read more and more stories from around the world, Molly began to notice recurring patterns in the stories. By imitating those patterns, she learned how to write stories of her own. Molly says, "Folktales are a beautiful, jewel-like form of writing. Emotions are never stated, but they are made clear by the actions of the characters. It's about as concise a story as a person can make."

In addition to writing and illustrating her own books, Molly spends time teaching art to children in schools. She believes that everyone can enjoy making art. "It's as if people think that artists and writers are these strange people who get their ideas beamed down from another planet," says Molly. "It's not as though we are different from anybody else. When I work with kids, the whole class works on projects together. Everybody contributes. Every child can write. Every child can make pictures that are special and quite wonderful."

DO IT YOURSELF!

Molly Bang suggests this activity for young writers: "All stories have some kind of pattern. With the help of a teacher, identify the pattern of a story. It's easy to identify the pattern in *Ten, Nine, Eight*. The pattern for *The Paper Crane* is: Man has a problem; stranger comes; man is kind to stranger; stranger solves problem. Make up your own story, following the basic pattern."

Shonto Begay

Born: February 7, 1954, in Shonto, Arizona
Home: Kayenta, Arizona

SELECTED TITLES

The Mud Pony
1988

Ma'ii and Cousin Horned Toad
1992

The Boy Who Dreamed of an Acorn
1994

The Magic of Spider Woman
1996

Navajo: Visions and Voices Across the Mesa
1996

A gentle-voiced man, Shonto Begay grew up on a Navajo reservation in the northeast corner of Arizona. The fifth of 16 children born to a Navajo medicine man, Shonto describes living in the earthen hogan (a building made of logs and mud): "I grew up with no television, no running water, no electricity," Shonto explains. "The hogan is about 20 feet in diameter, with an earth floor. Everybody sleeps in there. You roll open the sheepskin bedding in the evening. In the morning, after you've slept, you roll it back up. All the living is done in the hogan. If you want privacy, you go into the canyons, up to the mesa.

"I grew up tending sheep, staying with the flock all day, riding the horse in the valley, tending the cornfield in the summertime. By the time you got home in the evening, you were really tired so you would just eat and fall asleep. I didn't know there was any other lifestyle outside, beyond the horizons. I thought everybody in the world lived like this. It was normal."

Shonto's father, a well-respected man in the Native American community, made a living through his work as a healer. Shonto's mother, like most Navajo women of the time, was a weaver. Shonto's grandmother and grandfather also played vital roles in everyday family life.

Shonto recalls, "I grew up listening to my grandmother tell coyote stories. With the fire roaring in an old drum stove, shadows flickering in strange dances on the hogan walls, we listened intently as, with animated gestures and disguised voices, she made us laugh."

Shonto offers, "A lot of our teachings are explained through stories. I think all the Indian stories have messages in them, as opposed to television and other mass-produced forms of entertainment that don't have much redeeming value. Also, stories provide a verbal, historical account of one's identity. For a

group of people—a tribe or any other race—stories are one way to preserve a good portion of your culture."

While herding sheep as a child, Shonto would often go to a favorite place he called his story rock, where he could be alone with his thoughts and dreams. Shonto recalls, "There was one particular place atop the mesa where an outcropping of rock overlooks the whole valley . . . . I would sit there because it was always warmed by the sun in the winter and buffeted by cool air in the summer. I would read my storybooks—folktales, Mark Twain, Jack London."

> **"Everybody has a culture and an identity that they can draw strength from. Everybody's cultural background is valid and he or she should be proud of it."**

All his life, Shonto has felt a kinship with nature. He observes, "I grew up in a religion that reveres the earth. Every prayer begins: Mother Earth, Father Sky. The earth is treated just like the mother." The natural world—patterns in the sand, piñon pines bending in the wind, scattered pieces of driftwood—called out to Shonto as if asking to be drawn. Shonto says, "Looking at nature,

one can't help but feel compelled to create."

A Different World

Shonto first experienced life outside his own culture when, at the age of four, he went to the Bureau of Indian Affairs boarding school. He learned English and discovered such conveniences as electric lights and modern plumbing.

THE MUD PONY

Retold by Caron Lee Cohen
Illustrated by Shonto Begay

SCHOLASTIC

When he was old enough, Shonto set out to see the world beyond the horizon. After two years on the road, he ended up in Oakland, California. Shonto remembers: "I thought, This is really great. No more chopping wood, no more hauling water, no more being out in the cold. It was exciting, but it sort of wore off after a couple of years. Then I longed to get back to my animals, my home."

After seven years away from his homeland, Shonto returned. One day, out of the blue, he was contacted by an editor looking for a Native American artist to illustrate a Pawnee tale called *The Mud Pony*. Shonto gladly accepted the challenge. His career as a children's book illustrator, and later as a writer, had begun.

DO IT YOURSELF!

Shonto offers this advice to children: "Turn off the TV once in a while. Go a day without it. There are so many exciting things that are happening. All it takes is a walk alone, studying and observing nature." Why not try it—go a day (or a week!) without television. Like Shonto Begay, you may find your own story rock, a place to be alone with your thoughts and dreams.

Aliki Brandenberg

Born: September 3, 1929, in Wildwood Crest, New Jersey
Home: London, England

Aliki (pronounced "A-leekee") Brandenberg grew up in Philadelphia, the third of four children. "My parents were born in Greece," she says. "We spoke Greek in the house. We had Greek friends and Greek customs and ate Greek food. I was two people—I was Greek inside the house and I was American when I went to school."

When she was in kindergarten, Aliki's teacher told her parents, "Your daughter will be an artist one day." Aliki remembers, "I was always drawing, all through my life. I was just lucky to have a teacher who recognized my talent. When you are young, it's called talent; later on it becomes hard work and perseverance."

The subjects of Aliki's books range from dinosaurs to mummies, from medieval feasts to friendship and feelings. She even wrote a book about making books. Aliki says, "My writing takes two distinct directions. I write fiction, which comes from within, and nonfiction 'research books' about subjects that I want to learn more about.

"Writing and illustrating books," she says, "is a way of satisfying my curiosity. I'm just lucky that children are curious about the same things I am."

But where does Aliki find all those ideas? "Everything that I write comes from inside of me. My nonfiction books come from an interest in something, like the book *Mummies Made in Egypt*," she says. "I had never seen mummified animals before I visited the British Museum. I became so interested, I thought I'd write a book about the wrapping process. I read and read and read, did all my research, and found out everything except why mummies are wrapped in those patterns. That's the way it happens sometimes."

The way Aliki describes it, book ideas slowly take shape in the back of her mind, like bread dough rising. Suddenly an experience or remark will trigger an idea. She explains, "When we moved to London from New York, I missed my family and friends. Then a

friend remarked that her little boy drew pictures to send to his friend who had moved away. That inspired the book *We Are Best Friends*."

"I call my work hard fun. It's something I love and need to do, like breathing. I love the challenge that each day brings—the hard part as much as the fun part."

Another book, *The Two of Them*, is her most personal. "I wrote it when my father died. The child in the story is a cross between my daughter, Alexa, and myself. It's really told through her eyes. The ring in the book, for instance, is the ring that my father made when she was born. I wrote that book just to get my feelings out."

Back to the Drawing Board

Once Aliki has an idea, the hard work really begins. "I work at least 12 hours a day," she admits. "I can sit for eight hours at my desk without even thinking about food. And I can stay in my house for eight days without going out!"

For Aliki, the words come before the pictures. "Even though I have visual images while I am writing, they very often don't turn out the way I thought." Sometimes the

words come easily. But other times it's a struggle. Here's how Aliki solves writer's block: "If I can't get a story the way I want it, I put it aside for a time and do something else. Then I go back and see it with new eyes."

Sometimes Aliki will share her problems with an editor. "My editor at Greenwillow, Susan Hirschman, helped me very much with the book *Feelings*. I wrote it, but when it came time to do the illustrations I didn't know how to do it. I said to her, 'I don't think you want this book anymore because I don't know how to illustrate it.' But she said, 'You don't have to make big pictures—you can make little pictures.' That one comment helped me so much."

Aliki has also illustrated a number of books written by her husband, Franz Brandenberg. When she's not writing or illustrating books, Aliki loves gardening, films, traveling, baking, and reading. But Aliki is so busy, she admits that she doesn't find time to read as much as she would like. So, she says, "I go to the mountains, take a stack of books, and read for my vacation."

DO IT YOURSELF!

If you hope to become an artist, you can practice by drawing pictures of your toes. Aliki did. "I used to draw my toes all the time. And my feet. They were very hard to draw. I couldn't draw my hands as easily, because I was using them. So I drew my feet."

Jan Brett

Born: December 1, 1949, in Hingham, Massachusetts
Home: Norwell, Massachusetts

For Jan Brett, drawing and dreaming are almost the same thing. It is Jan's special time—a gift to the imagination, a time for daydreams. The everyday world falls away as she creates a new world, inch by inch, with her detailed illustrations. Jan describes the experience: "I like to put a lot of detail in my work. I work until I feel I've created a world that is possible to walk into. I like to get lost in the place that I'm creating. It's a lot like being in a happy dream."

Jan was a shy child. Uncomfortable with large groups of children, she preferred the company of pencil and paper. She recalls, "I spent hours drawing every day, because that's what I loved to do. If you had gone to my kindergarten class and asked me what I wanted to be, I'd have said, 'A children's book illustrator.' That's all I've ever wanted to be."

As you can tell from her books, Jan loves animals and nature. "When I was little," Jan says, "I had many pets. We raised guinea pigs and rabbits and had a donkey and a horse, in addition to the usual dogs and cats. I'll never forget my pet chicken, Delly, who used to ride on my shoulders. Now these animals, along with many others, reappear in my books."

Blending Ideas

Jan's most famous book, *The Wild Christmas Reindeer*, came about in part because of Jan's horse, Westy. But as with most of Jan's book ideas, there wasn't only one source. Her book ideas come from a variety of places. "I've always imagined what the North Pole would look like. And I thought about it for so long, all of a sudden I thought, This has got to be a book!"

Jan wanted the story to be about an animal. She recalls, "When I started thinking about the North Pole, I couldn't wait to draw the reindeer. At the same time I was wondering what could happen to the reindeer, I was having a bothersome time with my horse, Westy. Westy isn't perfect, and I

was trying hard to make him obey. I noticed that if I was angry with him and lost my temper, things only got worse. But if I took a deep breath and spoke calmly, he would listen to me."

- -

"Writing a story is like going down a path in the woods. You follow the path. You don't worry about getting lost, you just go."

- -

Jan decided that her story would be about an elf who has to get Santa's reindeer ready for the long Christmas ride. She sketched out a rough version, or dummy, of the book. Those rough pictures, drawn in about two weeks, showed what was going to happen on each page. Then came the more challenging part—the six-month-long process of finishing the illustrations.

To complete the drawings, Jan had to find a model for Teeka, the elf in the story. Using real models, Jan believes, keeps her drawings fresh and makes the character seem more believable to the reader. That raised the obvious question: Where was she going to find an elf? Jan recalls, "One day my husband came home and said, 'Oh, I met a little girl who looks like an elf.' That's all he said. When I met her, she was one of those children who didn't talk at

all to people, but when she saw an animal she lit up."

Imagine that you were going to be a model for one of Jan's stories. First you'd go shopping with Jan because you'd need to wear the right clothes. Then you'd sit down with her and read the dummy version of the book together. You'd talk about how the character feels and maybe give Jan an idea or two. Then you'd act out the entire book: leaping, walking, sitting—doing everything the character might do. All the while, Jan would watch closely and take photographs.

As a child, Jan often felt frustrated by book illustrations that didn't give enough information. That's why she likes to put in all the little details. Jan often uses borders to get all her ideas into the book. She explains, "I draw borders when I have too many ideas. In *The Mitten*, the borders show Nicki trekking through the woods and scaring different animals out of their hiding places. When you turn a page in the book, you can see the animal that comes next."

DO IT YOURSELF!

Here's something fun to do. But first, listen to Jan Brett: "Everyone likes to draw what he or she loves or does the best. For example, the hedgehog is my favorite animal and I think you can tell—it comes out better than an animal I don't like as much." Now it's your turn. Draw a picture of something you love or know about. Like Jan Brett, you might find it helpful to take a closer look at the real thing before you start your drawing.

Norman Bridwell

Born: February 15, 1928, in Kokomo, Indiana
Home: Martha's Vineyard, Massachusetts

SELECTED TITLES

Clifford the Big Red Dog
(first in a series)
1962

The Witch Next Door
(first in a series)
1965

Clifford's Good Deeds
1975

Count on Clifford
1985

Clifford's Puppy Days
1994

Clifford's First Autumn
1997

A Tiny Family
1999

*The Cat and the Bird
in the Hat*
2000

When Norman Bridwell first created Clifford—a clumsy, oversized, well-intentioned dog—he accomplished much more than he had set out to do. After all, Norman was only trying to get a story published. Instead he created a legendary character that would endure through generations. Today Clifford the Big Red Dog has starred in more than 45 million books, translated into over 10 languages.

But Bridwell takes little credit for the Big Red Dog's, well, *enormous* popularity. He modestly claims, "I just happened to think of it and put it down on paper. Somebody else could have done it just as easily. Luck had a lot to do with it."

Oddly enough, nobody made much of a fuss about Norman Bridwell's artistic talent when he was a child. He recalls, "I wasn't the one who got noticed. There was always somebody else singled out for praise. And it bothered me. But I didn't stop drawing. It was what I enjoyed doing."

After attending art school in Indiana, Bridwell moved to New York City. He found work as a commercial artist, working on a variety of projects. Still, he longed to try his hand at children's book illustration. "I did about ten sample paintings," Bridwell says. "I took these pictures around to 15 different publishers. Everywhere I went, I got the same reaction: *No response at all!*"

It was like his early school days all over again. No one seemed to notice, much less praise, Norman's artwork. One day an editor gave Norman a powerful piece of advice. He recalls the moment vividly: "She said, 'You're not very good. Your artwork is very ordinary.' But she suggested that I try my hand at writing too. She pointed to one sample picture, which was of a little girl with a great big dog (he was horse-sized in those days), and she said, 'Maybe that's a story.'"

That night, Norman went home and thought it over. He stared

at the drawing and let his imagination wander. In three days he wrote a story about Clifford and a young girl named Emily Elizabeth, named after Bridwell's own infant daughter.

> *"In school, my drawings were never the ones that were put on the board. But if you enjoy it, just keep doing it."*

Bridwell admits to complete shock when Scholastic decided to publish the book. "I was floored," Bridwell recalls, laughing at the memory. "I told my wife, Norma, 'Now don't count on there being any more. This is just a fluke. I don't know if there will ever be another one.'"

Today Bridwell remains humbled by his good fortune. Like his books, Norman is clear and direct, kind and gracious. He feels, he says, like an ordinary man who has been extraordinarily blessed. "Never in my wildest dreams could I have imagined that I would have such success," he says. "I'm extremely grateful to my readers and to the teachers who find Clifford useful for getting young readers started."

When pressed, Bridwell offers a few thoughts on Clifford's popularity. "He's well-meaning," Norman explains. "Clifford tries to be helpful. But he's also clumsy. He makes mistakes. He's not perfect. I think children appreciate the fact that perfect is not for everybody. We all have flaws."

When he speaks with children, Norman remembers the schoolboy he once was. He remembers the young artist whose drawings were never picked to go up on the wall. He remembers the young man in the big city, whose artwork was rejected by so many editors.

He explains, "I try to leave children with the idea that if they feel like doing something creative—if they like to make up stories, or if they like to draw—THEN DO IT. Don't be the sort of person who says, 'If I'm not the best, then I'm not going to do this anymore.' Try not to think about the other people getting the praise. Just do it for yourself. Because if only one person likes it, then you've done the right thing. I hate it when people shout, 'We're number one! We're number one!' You don't have to be number one. You can be someplace back in the pack, quietly doing something you love."

DO IT YOURSELF!

The advice that changed Norman Bridwell's life was simple. An editor pointed to a picture and said, "Maybe that's a story." Try it for yourself. Look at your own pictures or those in magazines. See if you can invent a story based on a picture.

Marc Brown

Born: November 25, 1946, in Erie, Pennsylvania
Home: Hingham, Massachusetts

Need a new idea? Try looking around. That's what Marc Brown does. "There are wonderful ideas for stories all around," says Marc. "All you have to do is keep your eyes and your ears open!"

Whenever Marc has time, he loves to visit children in schools. For him, it is a way to connect with his readers. It helps Marc remember his own days in school. During these visits, he often finds material he can use in his own writing. "After all," Marc admits, "practically all of my characters come from third grade."

When Marc steps into a school, he is all eyes and ears. "I go into overdrive," he says. "I find the day so exciting and intense. I'm like a sponge. There's all this great material everywhere. I try to remember it all."

When Marc gets an idea—it can be a picture, a snippet of conversation, the name of a character, even a book title—he stores it away until the time is right for that idea to "grow up" to become a book. Sometimes it takes years.

Marc explains, "My ideas have to germinate a long time before they come together in a book. I depend on drawers full of scraps of stories, bits of dialogue, quick drawings, titles, concepts. At any one time there are probably 100 ideas in the drawer, not all of them good."

Creating Arthur

Marc Brown is most famous for creating the character Arthur. Arthur was born when Marc began telling bedtime stories to his son, Tolon. Marc remembers, "Most of the stories were about animals. One night our story was about an aardvark who hated his nose. The aardvark, of course, was Arthur. That bedtime story became *Arthur's Nose*, the first book in the Arthur adventure series."

It's not easy coming up with new story ideas for Arthur, but Marc gets plenty of help from students and teachers. "*Arthur Meets the President* was suggested by a

teacher," Marc says. "As soon as she said it—that Arthur should visit the White House—three separate ideas came together. I'd always wanted to do a book on the White House. I'd also wanted to do a book about a field trip. And I'd wanted to do one about Arthur winning a contest. I just didn't know how to do it. Suddenly all those half-formed ideas came together."

"I am thrilled by children's reactions to my books. That's what fuels me to write other books."

Marc studied to be a painter in school. Maybe that's why he thinks that writing is a lot more difficult than drawing. "The writing is the hardest part," Marc admits. "It's something I have to do in order to get to the part I like." He adds with a laugh, "I wish someone else would do it for me, so I could just draw the pictures and have fun!"

Difficult or not, Marc realizes that writing gives him a chance to explore his own feelings. "When I wrote *Arthur's Eyes*, I was going through a divorce. The story happened to be about an aardvark getting glasses, but when I finished I realized it was really about adjusting to a whole new life. It was about trying something new, getting used to new things. It was about me."

Marc offers, "The book I'm proudest of is *Dinosaurs Divorce*. When I was first divorced, my two sons stayed with me. But all the books in the library showed the kids living with their mom. The dads would all go off to a hotel. My kids wondered what was wrong with our divorce." Working with his second wife, Laurene, Marc set out to write a book that would give children practical information about divorce. He says, "Every family divorces differently. Some ways, of course, are better than others, but there's no one right way."

Marc often discusses *Dinosaurs Divorce* when he visits classrooms. He says, "Afterward, kids who are going through a divorce come up to me. They just have to talk about it." Marc feels it's essential for children to express their feelings. He explains, with a hint of frustration in his voice, "We are so bad at letting people talk about their feelings. We are so afraid. What's wrong with us? They are just feelings— and they can hurt you if you don't talk about them."

MARC BROWN
ARTHUR MEETS THE PRESIDENT

AN ARTHUR ADVENTURE

DO IT YOURSELF!

Imagine that you are Marc Brown. It's your job to come up with an interesting story about Arthur. Remember, Marc has already written many Arthur books, so it won't be easy thinking up something exciting and new. When you've finished your story, you might want to send it with a letter to Marc.

Ashley Bryan

Born: July 13, 1923, in New York, New York
Home: Islesford, Maine

SELECTED TITLES

The Ox of the Wonderful Horns and Other African Folktales
1971

Walk Together Children: Black American Spirituals
1974

The Dancing Granny
1977

Beat the Story-Drum, Pum-Pum
1980

I'm Going to Sing: Black American Spirituals
1982

The Cat's Purr
1985

Lion and the Ostrich Chicks and Other African Folktales
1986

What a Morning! The Christmas Story in Black Spirituals
1987

All Night, All Day: A Child's First Book of African-American Spirituals
1991

Remembering his many visits to schools, Ashley Bryan says, "Kids often ask if I've won awards. I say, 'Yes, I have won awards.' But I also talk about when I did my first ABC book, in kindergarten. My mamma hugged and kissed me. My father spun me around. My sisters and brothers said, 'Hooray, Ashley!' My teacher said, 'You are the author, the illustrator, the binder. And when you take it home, you are the distributor too!' When I told her about the reception I got at home, she said, 'Well, you are getting rave reviews for that book of yours. So let's keep on publishing books!'

"That reaction," Ashley warmly recalls, "is still the greatest award I've ever received—the response of family, friends, neighbors, and teachers. It's an award children can experience themselves. I tell kids, 'Now is the time of great awards.'"

Ashley Bryan seeks treasures from the ancient days of Africa and brings them back for modern-day children to enjoy. But his treasures aren't gold coins or rare jewels. They are the folk stories once told by African people.

"Stories are always a treasury of the history of a people," Ashley says. "African tales are a beautiful means of linking the living Africa, past and present, to our own present. What the African sees in his world, the questions he asks, and the things that he feels and imagines have all found their way into the stories."

> **"I hope that my work with the African tales will be, by the very nature of storytelling, like a tender bridge reaching us across distances of time and space."**

Spending long hours in libraries, Ashley Bryan searches in scholarly books for African folktales. He then retells those stories in his own words, hoping to bring them alive for a new generation of readers.

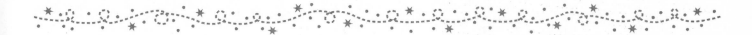

Ashley explains, "When I write, I'm trying to find the sound of the voice in the printed word. That's what I'm always after. I'm usually working from forms that simply document the basic story. They may be just a few sentences or just a paragraph or two. They were not intended to convey anything of what it is when you tell a story. I look at those words and say, 'Nobody would tell a story like that!'"

Ashley's job as he sees it is to recapture the spirit of the original stories. He says, "I want to get across the feeling of the storyteller so that the person reading it will feel the presence of the storyteller." In this way, Ashley's written stories capture the mood of the period in which the stories were first told— a time when a circle of people gathered around the storyteller.

Writing With the Ear

According to Ashley, the ear is an important element of a story. That's because he works within the storytelling tradition, where there is always a voice to speak the words and an ear to hear them. The sound of spoken words, he believes, is like a song. And he always tries to make that song as beautiful as possible.

Ashley says, "My first version states the basic story. I will then try speaking it, hearing it. Then I'll go on to a second version, a third, a fourth. At each stage I will test it

with my voice. Then I'll go back to the writing. By the time I reach a fifth version, it begins to have its own voice. Finally, the story reaches the point where I can say to it, 'You are alive!'"

If Ashley Bryan seems particularly fond of the sound of words, it might be because he inherited a love of music from his parents. "One of my earliest recollections is of my mother singing. She sang from one end of the day to the other. My father used to say, 'Son, your mother must think she's a bird.' My father loved birds. The living rooms of our various Bronx apartments were always lined with shelves, not for books but for birds. Once I counted over a hundred birds in his collection. My mother used to say, 'If I want any attention around here, I'll have to get in a cage.'"

Beat the Story-Drum, Pum-Pum

by ASHLEY BRYAN

DO IT YOURSELF!

Imagine that you are a time traveler from the year 2199, and that your job is to study the people of Earth today. One way to do this is by asking people to tell you stories about their lives. Be sure to write them down. Think about what their stories reveal about the thoughts, feelings, and values of the strange culture you're studying.

Eve Bunting

Born: December 19, 1928, in Haghera, Northern Ireland
Home: Pasadena, California

SELECTED TITLES

How Many Days to America?
1988

The Wednesday Surprise
1989

The Wall
1990

Fly Away Home
1991

The Day Before Christmas
1992

Someday a Tree
1993

A Day's Work
1994

Night of the Gargoyles
1994

Smoky Night
(Caldecott Medal)
1994

Going Home
1996

Ducky
1997

The Memory String
2000

For Eve Bunting, the writing process is a thinking process. In fact, Eve rarely touches pencil to paper (Eve prefers writing first drafts by hand) until the story is clearly formed in her mind. Eve calls this thought process the planning stage and considers it about 95 percent of her writing process.

Eve explains, "One of the blessings in my life—that could be a curse, I suppose—is that I'm a total insomniac. A great deal of my thinking is done either when I'm out on one of my daily long walks or when I'm sleepless. I will not put a word down until I have that picture book pretty much gelled in my mind. And I certainly always have the first two paragraphs, word for word, in my mind. Those words will probably not ever change. And I always have the ending—definitely the last sentence, because that to me is what's packing the whallop in my picture book."

Eve uses her award-winning book *The Wall* as an example. For a long while, Eve knew she wanted to write a story centered on the Vietnam War Memorial. She even knew the message of her story. But Eve didn't have the beginning—those first few lines that act like a door opening, allowing the writer into the story.

"Writing is like breathing. It's just plain necessary."

"It took me three years to get the first three lines of that book," Eve recounts. "I kept thinking about it and thinking about it, just getting really irritated with myself and irritated with the idea. I never abandoned it, mind you, but I put it on the back burner. Then when I woke up one morning, I had the lines for it: *This is the wall. My grandfather's wall. On it are the names of those killed in a war long ago.*"

Eve continues, "The minute I had those lines, I got right up out of bed. I sat down before breakfast and wrote those three lines. Then the first draft of the entire book

was done in about two hours. I'd been working on it in my subconscious for three years, actually!"

Eve Bunting was born and raised in Northern Ireland. You can still hear an Irish lilt in her voice. In 1958, at age 30, Eve immigrated to California with her husband and three children. But she never left the old country far behind; her essential "Irishness" remains. For Ireland is a land of words—of lively talk, long stories, and uproarious laughter. And Eve Bunting is Irish to the bone: She grew up loving the sound of words, thanks in great part to her parents, both of whom were ardent book lovers.

As a schoolgirl, Eve enjoyed writing so much she often volunteered to do her friends' writing homework! Eve confesses, "I thought writing was fun! But I never thought of it as a profession. I'd never actually tried to sell anything—or thought of writing in that way at all—until I came onto middle age."

After she left high school at age 17, Eve didn't write creatively for more than 20 years. Then, almost on a whim, Eve took a writing class at a local university. Instantly, the floodgates opened. Stories have been pouring out of Eve at a torrential rate ever since. Today she is easily one of the most prolific writers in children's literature, with nearly 200 books published.

"Getting ideas is never my problem," Eve confesses. "My problem is that the world is filled with so many ideas and here am I, right smack in the middle of it. I couldn't possibly write about all the interesting things I see around me or all the interesting thoughts that pop into my head. There aren't that many hours in a day or that many days in a year."

There doesn't seem to be any subject that Eve won't tackle. As she puts it, "I've written of kings and princes, and of ordinary children growing up, and of young men growing old. I've written of happy families and unhappy families, of living and dying."

Eve Bunting has shown a unique ability to face serious issues head-on, ranging from homelessness to the plight of boat people. Eve writes about whatever moves her, whether it makes her laugh or cry. She concludes, "As a writer, you have to be open to what's going on—and not be afraid of it. I think adults tend not to understand how smart children are. I never write down to children in my books. I think they understand more, and are more sensitive, than an awful lot of adults give them credit for."

EVE BUNTING
Illustrated by
DAVID DIAZ

DO IT YOURSELF!

Eve Bunting offers this advice to young writers: "Open your eyes to what's all around you, because ideas are floating in the air. You just have to grab them and pull them in. Sometimes they are not worth it; then you just set them free again for some other author to take care of! And be aware of other people's feelings. Don't just think of yourself all the time. And if you do that, then, well, ideas will come!"

Eric Carle

Born: June 25, 1929, in Syracuse, New York
Home: Northampton, Massachusetts

SELECTED TITLES

Brown Bear, Brown Bear
1967

The Very Hungry Caterpillar
1969

The Tiny Seed
1970

Do You Want to Be My Friend?
1971

The Grouchy Ladybug
1977

The Very Busy Spider
1984

Papa, Please Get the Moon for Me
1986

The Very Quiet Cricket
1990

Draw Me a Star
1992

Today Is Monday
1993

The Art of Eric Carle
1996

Does a Kangaroo Have a Mother, Too?
2000

O f all the questions kids ask Eric Carle, "Where do ideas come from?" is the one he hears most often. Although Eric thinks it would take hours to fully answer, he offers this explanation: "Of course, the question of where ideas come from is the most difficult of all. Some people like to say they get ideas when they're in the shower. That's always a very entertaining answer, but I think it's much deeper than that. It goes back to your upbringing, your education, and so forth." For Eric, ideas don't come from one place. They come from all the experiences in his life, all the thoughts in his mind, and all the feelings in his heart.

A Bridge to America

Eric Carle was born in Syracuse, New York, to German immigrants. When he was six, he and his parents moved back to Germany. Eric hated the strict discipline of his new German school. Sad and confused, he longed to return to America. A fantasy grew inside him: "When it became apparent that we would not return, I decided that I would become a bridge builder. I would build a bridge from Germany to America and take my beloved German grandmother by the hand across the wide ocean."

It would be 17 years before Eric returned. In a sense, this difficult period was a significant source of inspiration for Eric's later books. As an artist, Eric strives to help children enjoy school more than he did. He says, "I am fascinated by the period in a child's life when he or she, for the first time, leaves home to go to school. I should like my books to bridge that great divide."

Growing up, Eric loved to walk through the woods with his father. He fondly recalls, "He'd turn over a rock and show me the little creatures that scurried and slithered about." On these walks, filled with laughter and discovery, Eric learned to love nature. Giving us another clue to where he finds his ideas, Eric

says, "I try to recall that feeling when I write my books."

Sometimes ideas for Eric's books come from just fooling around. At least that's how he describes the inception of *The Very Hungry Caterpillar*. "I playfully punched a hole into a stack of papers. I thought, A bookworm at work! Not enough for a book, but, nevertheless, a beginning."

"I want children to know that learning can be fun, delightful, interesting, silly."

Eventually, Eric submitted his story about the bookworm, who had been changed to a green worm named Willy. His editor liked the idea—almost. She asked, "How about a caterpillar?" And so Eric Carle's most famous book was born.

By the way, Eric already knows that a caterpillar emerges from a chrysalis, not a cocoon! So don't bother writing to tell him. Eric explains how the famous "mistake" crept into the book: "My editor contacted a scientist, who said that it was permissible to use the word *cocoon*. Poetry over science. It simply would not have worked to say 'Come out of your chrysalis!' If we can accept giants tied down by dwarfs, genies in bottles, and knights who attack windmills, why can't a caterpillar

come out of a cocoon?"

The most important part of developing a book, Eric believes, is working with editors to revise it. He says, "You

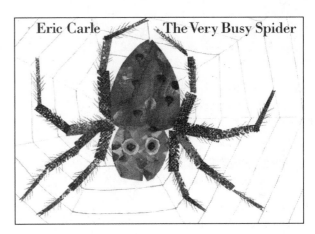

Eric Carle   The Very Busy Spider

have doubts. You hate it. You love it. You discuss it with your editors. You change it. Finally, at one point you just know it's right. After that it goes very quickly. The art for *The Tiny Seed* took only two weeks!"

So where *do* ideas come from? Eric likes the answer his Uncle August used to give. "I'd say, 'Uncle August, tell me a story.' Peering over his glasses he'd say, 'First you have to wind up my thinking machine.' And, as I had done many times before, I began to wind an imaginary lever near his temple. After a little while—all along he had made whirring noises—he shouted, 'Halt! I have a story for you!'"

Eric says, "I like my Uncle August's answer to where stories come from. They come from your thinking machine. All you have to do is wind it up."

DO IT YOURSELF!

Team up with a friend to write and illustrate your own version of *The Very Hungry Caterpillar*. Follow the original pattern of the book but make a few key changes. (The Very Hungry Monster? The Very Sleepy Puppy? The Very Naughty Student?)

Joanna Cole

Born: August 11, 1944, in Newark, New Jersey
Home: Sandy Hook, Connecticut

Selected Titles

A Frog's Body
1980

Bony-Legs
1983

Cars and How They Go
1983

How You Were Born
1984

The Magic School Bus at the Waterworks
(first in a series)
1986

Evolution
1987

Bully Trouble
1989

Don't Call Me Names
1990

My Puppy Is Born
1991

Six Sick Sheep: 101 Tongue Twisters
1993

The Gator Girls
(first in a series)
1995

What's Joanna Cole interested in? Well, just about everything! And when Joanna Cole is interested in something, she usually writes a book about it. She's written about fleas, cockroaches, dinosaurs, chicks, fish, saber-toothed tigers, frogs, horses, snakes, cars, puppies, insects, and (whew!) babies.

"I was never one of those wonderful students who gets straight A's and everything right on the tests," says Joanna Cole. "But I've always been obsessed with logical thinking. I used to argue with my teachers when things didn't make sense to me."

Joanna grew up in East Orange, New Jersey. Her interest in science grew from her natural curiosity about the world in which she lived. "We had a small backyard, and I was the gardener in the family. I spent a lot of time planting flowers, daydreaming, watching ants, and catching bugs."

It Began With Cockroaches

All writers must begin somewhere, and Joanna Cole began her career by writing about cockroaches.

Joanna was working as a library teacher in a Brooklyn elementary school when her father gave her an article. Joanna remembers, "It was about cockroaches and how they were here before the dinosaurs. It got me thinking about all those science books I'd read as a kid—insects had been a special interest of mine—and it occurred to me that there wasn't one about cockroaches."

As a nonfiction writer, Joanna does a lot of research before she writes a single word. "The impossible dream is to know everything," she says. "When you are writing the book, you must select what you want to go into the book. What always happens is that more things are left out than can go in.

"I have a question that I ask myself as I write: Why does the reader want to turn the page? I never feel that kids are going to turn the page just because it's there to turn. There has to be a

question that's in a reader's mind—and he or she turns the page to find the answer.

"Kids often ask me if it's fun to be a writer. That question always leaves me a little speechless, because the answer is, of course, yes and no. When it's going well, there's nothing more exhilarating. But it's so much work!"

> **"When I'm writing a book, it's almost as if I'm building a cabinet. I want it all to fit together. I work very hard at that."**

Joanna has been praised by both teachers and children for being able to make science interesting and understandable. And now, with the Magic School Bus series, Joanna has done the impossible— she's made science funny.

"Before I started writing the first Magic School Bus book, I had a lot of lofty goals—and I had no idea whether they could be achieved. I wanted it to be a very good science book. I also wanted it to be a good story, a story you might read even without the science. And I wanted it to be genuinely funny. Well, this was terrifying to me. I couldn't work at all. I cleaned out closets, answered letters, went shopping— anything but sit down and write. But eventually I did it, even though I was scared."

The Magic School Bus books were

a huge success. Readers across the country loved them. They especially loved the wacky science teacher, Ms. Frizzle. "We were concerned that teachers might be offended by Ms. Frizzle, with her crazy clothes. But what's happened is that teachers love her. Whenever Bruce Degen, the illustrator, and I go to schools, there's almost always somebody dressed as Ms. Frizzle. The teachers are even asking for Ms. Frizzle outfits."

In addition to her many science books, Joanna Cole has written over 20 books of fiction including *Don't Tell the Whole World, The Clown-Arounds, Bony-Legs, Doctor Change, Monster Manners,* and *The Missing Tooth.*

Joanna Cole finds pleasure and excitement in each new project she takes on. "When I was starting to write *The Magic School Bus Inside the Human Body,* I didn't know whose body the bus would travel in. Then I thought of the idea that Ms. Frizzle and her class would go into Arnold's body, and that he would eat them as Cheesie Wheesies. That was one of the happiest moments of my life. I was walking on clouds all day."

DO IT YOURSELF!

Joanna Cole says kids sometimes write their own Magic School Bus adventures. Here's her advice: "Start by picking a topic and a place for the field trip. Do a lot of research. Think of a story line—and come up with lots of jokes. Some kids like to put their own teacher and class into the story."

Barbara Cooney

Born: August 6, 1917, in Brooklyn, New York
Home: Damariscotta, Maine

SELECTED TITLES

Chanticleer and the Fox
(Caldecott Medal)
1958

Ox-Cart Man
(Caldecott Medal)
1979

Miss Rumphius
1982

*The Story of Holly
and Ivy*
1985

Island Boy
1988

*The Year of the Perfect
Christmas Tree*
1988

*Hattie and the
Wild Waves*
1990

Emily
1992

Letting Swift River Go
1992

Only Opal
1994

Eleanor
1996

Basket Moon
1999

It is snowing in Damariscotta, Maine. A foot has fallen since the previous night, and now a soft white blanket covers Barbara Cooney's world. "It's wonderful," Barbara says as she looks up at the skylights of her attic studio. "It's lovely to sit here and watch the weather come down." Barbara has already taken a long morning walk in the snow and now she's ready to talk about her work.

"Of all the books I have done," Barbara says, "*Miss Rumphius, Island Boy,* and *Hattie and the Wild Waves* are closest to my heart. They are as near as I ever will come to an autobiography."

Barbara Cooney published her first book in 1940, more than 60 years ago. Though she has won two Caldecott Medals, she says she is proudest of the work that came after those books were published—after Barbara reached an age, in fact, when most people quit work and retire. Barbara tells us, "I knew I had to change after *Ox-Cart Man.* I mean, how many medals do you need to make you feel that you've finished your apprenticeship?" She adds with confidence: "I think I've done my best work in the last 20 years, starting with *Miss Rumphius.*"

> *"Sometimes you look at your work on the drawing board, and it's like a battlefield. You are fighting to get the picture to turn out right."*

Stitching together pieces from her own life—and the life of her family—Barbara wrote a story about a young girl named Alice Rumphius who was determined to accomplish three things when she grew up: She would visit faraway places, she would live by the sea, and she would do something to make the world more beautiful.

Barbara notes, "People really latched onto the message. Children write letters to me about what they are going to do to make the world better." But, she is

quick to say, "I wasn't trying to preach at all—I would never do that. Basically I took episodes from my life and made a story."

Blending Fact With Fiction

Near her home in Maine, Barbara had heard a story about a woman called the Lupine Lady. "She lived in this area and used to go around throwing lupine seeds all over the place. She gets a lot of credit for these wild fields of lupine around here. I thought, Well, that's a nice thing to peg a story on, but I didn't know how to do it. Then one day I sat down and embellished the idea with memories of my mother, my grandmother, my great-grandfather, and my travels."

Like Miss Rumphius, Barbara enjoyed many adventures during her own travels. She relates, "I've done lots and lots of traveling to all sorts of exotic places. Really, that book would have been twice as long if my editor had let me put in all the places I wanted to draw and write about!"

After the success of *Miss Rumphius*, Barbara went on to illustrate more books by other authors. But she soon returned to a subject close to her heart. "*Island Boy* is my hymn to Maine," she confides.

Last in Barbara's trilogy is *Hattie and the Wild Waves*, the story of a young girl who follows her dream to become an artist. While the

facts of the story are based upon her mother's life, Barbara confesses: "I think Hattie is probably me."

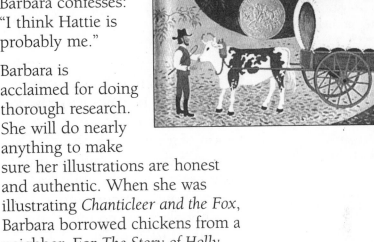

Barbara is acclaimed for doing thorough research. She will do nearly anything to make sure her illustrations are honest and authentic. When she was illustrating *Chanticleer and the Fox*, Barbara borrowed chickens from a neighbor. For *The Story of Holly and Ivy*, she visited England's Scotland Yard to find out how many buttons a policeman has on his uniform! And for *The Year of the Perfect Christmas Tree*, Barbara spent a week in the Appalachian Mountains climbing hills, visiting homes, getting props, observing how the setting sun lights the valley. It was a lot simpler to research *Ox-Cart Man*. She says with a laugh, "All I had to do was step outside my back door!"

How does Barbara Cooney describe what drives her to write? "I think what I'm doing is trying to communicate the things I love in the world, to make a record of what captivates me. With each photograph or drawing I say, 'Isn't this great? Isn't this delicious? Isn't this funny?'"

DO IT YOURSELF!

Read *Miss Rumphius*. Like Alice, think about what you might do to make the world a better place. Then do it! You might like to write about what you've done—and why.

Donald Crews

Born: August 30, 1938, in Newark, New Jersey
Home: Brooklyn, New York

Donald Crews collects ideas. One of his favorite activities is to wander around the city looking for images that excite and interest him. "I do it all the time," Crews says. "I don't think I'm ever without a camera and a sketchbook. I use both of them for collecting ideas."

At this point, camera in hand, Crews isn't thinking about making a book. Instead, he's seeking a beginning—an inspiration, an idea that may lead to another idea. "My images, or my ideas, are reality-based. They all start someplace—most likely with a photograph."

The subjects of his books are always drawn from real life. It may be a city parade, the memory of a childhood train journey, a carousel in an amusement park, or the flight of an airplane. His books remind us that everyday life is interesting and exciting—all you have to do is look closely.

Truck was inspired by living in the city near a commercial truck depot. Crews, always on the lookout for something visually exciting, became fascinated with the trucks. He remembers, "Each day trucks delivered and picked up all kinds of goods and performed all sorts of services. A lot of these trucks were red, and all had great typographic images on their sides."

Developing Ideas

How does Donald Crews develop an idea into a book? The process goes something like this: "Once I become fascinated with a subject, I'll do some freewheeling sketches. At that point I'm not really putting a book together, I'm just thinking it through and exploring the visual possibilities."

The next step is to create tiny thumbnail sketches. Donald says, "This way I can see, roughly, all 32 pages of the book. I'll know the sequence of events before I start to illustrate."

Words come next. But for Donald

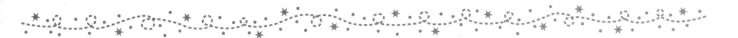

Crews, the central focus is always the pictures. "I'm not primarily a writer, and I think the pictures are more effective than the words," he states. "I'm continually paring down the number of words I'm using. I'm also trimming down and tightening up the illustrations to make them more effective.

"I took pictures of bicycle races for years, never thinking they'd be the subject of a book. But, eventually, those photos led to Bicycle Race."

"I really believe in the idea of a picture book. A picture book is a book that ought to tell the story with pictures. If it takes too many words to make it work, then it isn't a picture book anymore." With this in mind, Crews returns again and again to his text, revising and eliminating words.

The plot, or action of the book, may be surprisingly simple. A truck picks up a load and travels to its destination. A carousel takes on riders, revolves, and stops. By focusing on a simple action, Crews seeks to capture the excitement of the action. Sometimes he'll go to great lengths to achieve the effect of motion.

The book *Carousel* features some exciting pages that show all sorts

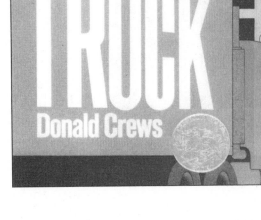

of blurred movement. "It's actually photography," Crews explains. "The primary illustration is a drawn-and-painted carousel. Then I took a series of color photographs of that piece of art, moving the camera to create the illusion of movement.

"I used that same idea, without a camera, for *Freight Train*. But in order to get the same kind of motion in a carousel—which is much more complicated in terms of drawing—I thought that photography would be a good way to do it." After many experiments (and several rolls of film), Crews finally achieved the effect he wanted.

Readers can look forward to many more books from Donald Crews. And with each one, it seems, comes a journey—on a plane, in a parade, on a freight train. But no matter where the journey leads, everyone is invited. All you have to do is pick up a book, bring your imagination, and climb aboard!

DO IT YOURSELF!

You can have a lot of fun making your own book based on the themes in Donald Crews's books. Take his book *Light*, for example. Draw your own pictures of lights, using familiar objects from your everyday life. Or choose another theme—soccer balls, skateboards, puppets, or whatever interests you.

Bruce Degen

Born: June 14, 1945, in Brooklyn, New York
Home: Newtown, Connecticut

SELECTED TITLES

Commander Toad in Space
(first in a series)
1980

Little Chick's Big Day
1981

Jamberry
1983

Jesse Bear, What Will You Wear?
(first in a series)
1986

The Josefina Story Quilt
1986

The Magic School Bus at the Waterworks
(first in a series)
1986

If You Were a Writer
1988

Dinosaur Dances
1990

Teddy Bear Towers
1991

Sailaway Home
1996

Daddy Is a Doodlebug
2000

Fantasy plays an important role in Bruce Degen's books. But each story or illustration, he says, begins with a close look at everyday life.

Bruce explains, "Even though my style is not strictly realistic, the shapes that I put into my drawings come from looking at real things. For instance, when I created *Commander Toad*, I first did pages and pages of research sketches on toads and frogs."

When creating a character, Bruce usually begins by making realistic drawings. Gradually, after completing many sketches, he'll add lots of personality to those realistic drawings. For Bruce Degen, the process clearly works; he's helped bring to life many memorable children's book characters: Commander Toad, Jesse Bear, the Forgetfuls, and, of course, Ms. Frizzle.

What's the most difficult thing about inventing a new character? Bruce admits, "The hardest thing to do is make it turn around—to draw it from the front and the side and still make it look like the same character." With a modest laugh, he confesses, "I don't always do that so well!"

Catching Ideas

As a helpful reference, Bruce keeps files of pictures that he's clipped from magazines. That way, if he needs to see a picture of a rabbit, he simply turns to the file. For one particular project, Bruce had to draw a mouse. He says, "I didn't have too many good pictures of mice in my files." Always creative, Bruce found a clever solution—in his basement!

He explains, "As it turns out, we had mice in the basement, so I went out and got a live trap. I caught a whole family of mice, and I've got them in a cage in the basement. Rather than have them running around chewing up things, we decided to have them as guests for the winter. We feed them, we talk to them, and I draw them. So I solved two problems at once!"

Bruce has written only a few of the many books he has illustrated, but he hopes to write more in the future. The problem is, he gets so much work as an illustrator there just aren't enough hours in the day to write! "I'm a very slow writer and a very fast illustrator," Bruce says. "Whenever I'm given a manuscript that's fun, I do that and forget about writing for a little while."

> **"Each of us has individual things that mean something to us, things that no one else is carrying around. That's a good jumping-off point for a story. It's a place to start."**

His best-loved book is undoubtedly the whimsical *Jamberry*. Even this fantasy story, he claims, has its foundations in real life. "*Jamberry* grew out of personal experience. You see, I grew up in a very urban part of the city. There was no grass or gardens, just sidewalks and cement. In the summer we used to go up to the Catskill Mountains, and it was totally the opposite. The world was generous. The berries were free, like a gift. When I wanted to do a book about being young and joyful, I remembered those berry-picking trips. I made up a nonsense rhyme using the names of berries. The point is, I started by pulling something out of my memory that meant something to me."

Bruce finds that by illustrating a book, he usually discovers new things about the story. "When I started *Jamberry*, I thought I was the little boy in the story. But halfway through the book, while I was doing the drawing of the boy and bear going over the waterfall in the canoe, I suddenly understood that I was the bear and the little boy was my son."

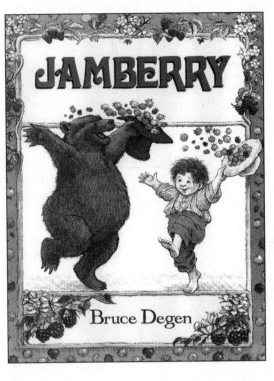

A lifelong New Yorker, Bruce moved to a new home in Connecticut in the early 1990s. It changed his working habits significantly. "When I lived in the city," he says, "I used to get on the subway and ride to my studio, stay there all day, and then come home. But now I work at home. In the morning I pick up my cup of coffee and say to my wife, 'I'm off to the office, dear!' and walk upstairs. It sure beats the subway."

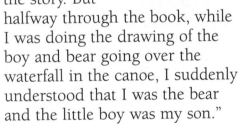

DO IT YOURSELF!

In *Jamberry*, Bruce made up a nonsense poem about his favorite food. Read *Jamberry* and then write your own silly poem. It could be about pizza, hamburgers, ice cream, or, hey, even spinach!

Lulu Delacre

Born: December 20, 1957, in Puerto Rico
Home: Silver Springs, Maryland

SELECTED TITLES

Nathan and Nicholas Alexander
(first in a series)
1986

Arroz Con Leche: Popular Songs and Rhymes From Latin America
1989

Las Navidades: Popular Christmas Songs From Latin America
1990

Vejigantes Masquerade
1993

The Bossy Gallito: A Traditional Cuban Folktale
1994

Golden Tales: Myths, Legends, and Folktales From Latin America
1996

Salsa Stories
2000

Lulu Delacre (pronounced De-LAK-ray) visited Miami, Florida. She walked the streets, sampled Cuban dishes, talked to many people, and took lots of pictures. Sounds like a nice vacation, doesn't it? But Lulu wasn't on vacation—she was doing research for a book!

"Research is a lot of fun," says Lulu. "That's when you learn. You get to talk to people, you get to see places, you get to take pictures and read wonderful books!"

Lulu travels great distances to visit the places she plans to feature in her books. While staying in these far-off cities, Lulu notices the clothes the people wear, the games they play, and the way a certain street looks in the sun-drenched afternoon light. She feels it's very important for each of her illustrations to be accurate. With these details, Lulu hopes to convey the subtle flavors of everyday life.

Lulu began her writing career with *Nathan and Nicholas Alexander*, a story about a gentle elephant that befriends a rather haughty mouse. Lulu, a wife and mother of two daughters, says, "Nathan is the son I never had." In all, she has created four books featuring these two unlikely friends.

Though Lulu has enjoyed the Nathan series, her bilingual books hold a special place in her heart. Perhaps that's because these books (*Arroz Con Leche, Las Navidades, Vejigantes Masquerade*) are closely connected to her own childhood.

Lulu explains, "Writing bilingual books has been the greatest challenge of my career. It's a big task, dealing with two languages—one of them my mother tongue—and portraying my own culture with authenticity in both words and pictures. It's also an important duty of which I feel very proud."

Celebrating Her Culture

From early childhood, Lulu has moved easily from one culture to another. She's had to: Her parents are from Argentina; she was born and raised in Puerto Rico; she studied art in France; and she now lives in Maryland!

But when Lulu went to the library to find books for her two daughters to read, she realized how hard it was to find children's books that represented her own Latin American culture. Lulu knew how to solve that problem, though—she'd write the books herself!

Lulu, who taught her two daughters to read in Spanish, continues, "I thought there had to be parents like me, who had children unfamiliar with their heritage. Many children, in order to integrate, try to forget their backgrounds. They don't learn their parents' language and folklore. I felt there was a need for a book that would provide a sample of my folklore and a positive image of the Latin American people."

Lulu hopes that children will value their families' traditions as well as the traditions of other cultures. "The more you know about another person's cultural heritage, the more you can understand why he or she acts certain ways. When you learn to appreciate other people's cultural and ethnic backgrounds, a positive energy develops that may lead to harmony."

Lulu Delacre dreams of a day when classrooms are full of children of different backgrounds who appreciate one another's differences. Lulu states, "We need to achieve that among all cultures—without forgetting our roots. We should celebrate the differences that make us unique."

Lulu enjoys visiting schools and working with children. She tells this story: "I conducted a picture-book workshop where I took 75 second-graders through the process of creating a children's book. I told them, 'You have to start with an idea. Well,' I asked, 'where do ideas come from? Why don't you write about something that you've lived, something that you've done— a day that was very sad, a day that was wonderful and happy. Write about something that has happened to you.'"

The author concludes: "It's much better to write about something you know than about something you don't know."

Tomie dePaola

Born: September 15, 1934, in Meriden, Connecticut
Home: New London, New Hampshire

SELECTED TITLES

The Cloud Book: Words and Pictures
1975

Strega Nona: An Old Tale
(Caldecott Honor Book)
1975

The Popcorn Book
1978

Francis, the Poor Man of Assisi
1982

The Legend of the Bluebonnet: An Old Tale of Texas
1983

Tomie dePaola's Mother Goose
1984

The Art Lesson
1989

Tom
1993

The Baby Sister
1996

26 Fairmount Avenue
(Newbery Honor Book)
1999

With nearly 200 books to his credit, Tomie dePaola (pronounced "de-POW-la") knows something about ideas. In fact, he's bursting with them. When he's working on one book, he's usually thinking about the next. He's never had writer's block, though he does confess to a single, brief bout with artist's block. For Tomie, the ideas keep flowing, book after book after book.

Tomie dePaola believes that many people give up on their ideas too easily. He says, "I think if you have an idea, you should hang on to it. Write it down and think about it for a while. Sometimes nothing happens with ideas. But some of them eventually become books."

The important thing about ideas, the prolific dePaola believes, is to explore them. "Ideas are like doors," he says. "It might just be a door that gets you to another door. But it might lead you to the secret door that opens up to the green meadow outside the castle."

According to dePaola, "We're not encouraged to take an idea that comes into our head and explore it to see if it's good or not. When a kid gets an idea that doesn't seem to fit into his teacher's or his parents' mode, they say, 'That's not a good idea.' An example is when my brother and I would have the idea of going to the amusement park. We would say, 'Can we go to the park?' My mother would respond, 'That's not a good idea.'

"But we, of course, thought it was a terrific idea. Instead of giving up on it, my brother and I would join forces. Suddenly we'd do the dishes, help around the house, and start dropping little hints. Eventually our parents would give in and we'd be taken to the amusement park. The whole process might take two or three weeks. The point is, we would work on the idea. We'd develop it. We'd say, 'Let's not give up this idea.'"

Feeding the Imagination

Although Tomie dePaola's books include nonfiction and fiction, he generally draws upon his childhood as a source of inspiration and guidance. An example can be found in his book *The Art Lesson*. Tomie recalls, "*The Art Lesson* is based on something that actually happened. I never forgot that incident. I had been telling that story for years when my editor, Margaret Frith, suggested that it might make a good book. So I sat down and wrote the same story I had been telling."

"I think going to the movies or taking a walk or cooking pizza is fun. Sitting down and doing books is not fun. It's my job. I take my job as seriously as I would if I were a brain surgeon."

To create his artwork, dePaola needs to be in his studio, surrounded by his beloved materials. "But," dePaola adds with a laugh, "that's not true for writing. I can write anywhere! I have written drafts of manuscripts on airplanes. It's easy. You just put on your Walkman, flip down the table, and write."

Tomie explains, "I do a first draft that no one sees but me. I do a lot of my writing in my head first, just thinking the story through. Usually it's a revised second draft that gets typed neatly and sent along to my editor. Then my editor reads it and makes suggestions. We often work on the final draft together. We sit down, side by side, and write together."

Tomie dePaola has had a lifelong interest in folktales. The tales may be Italian, Irish, African, or Native American in origin—it doesn't matter to dePaola, as long as it's a good story. According to him, all stories offer some insight into ourselves. He says, "I'm very into celebrating the differences between people. In celebrating ethnic differences, we often discover how much people are really the same. People are people. They all have feelings. Ultimately, native customs are all focused on the same thing—to help us learn about life."

Strega Nona's Magic Lessons

STORY AND PICTURES BY Tomie de Paola

DO IT YOURSELF!

Before he wrote about it, Tomie dePaola used to talk about the event that inspired his book *The Art Lesson*. Think of a real-life story that you would like to tell your friends. Instead of talking about it, write it down. After all, everybody has stories—but it's a writer who takes the time to put them down on paper.

Diane and Leo Dillon

Diane Dillon, **Born:** March 13, 1933, in Glendale, California
Leo Dillon, **Born:** March 2, 1933, in Brooklyn, New York
Home: Brooklyn, New York

SELECTED TITLES

*The Ring in the Prairie:
A Shawnee Legend*
1970

*Why Mosquitoes
Buzz in People's Ears:
A West African Tale*
(Caldecott Medal)
1975

*Ashanti to Zulu:
African Traditions*
(Caldecott Medal)
1976

*The People Could Fly:
American Black Folktales*
1985

The Porcelain Cat
1987

Aida
1990

*The Tale of the
Mandarin Ducks*
1990

The Sorcerer's Apprentice
1993

*The Girl Who Dreamed
Only Geese*
1997

*To Every Thing There
Is a Season*
1998

Are two heads better than one? Well, if the heads are Leo and Diane Dillon's, the answer is a resounding "Yes!"

Both Leo and Diane are gifted artists. But as Leo says, "Together we are able to create art we would not be able to do individually."

Leo explains the process this way: "Each illustration is passed back and forth between us several times before it is completed, and since we both work on every piece of art, the finished painting looks as if one artist has done it."

Diane agrees: "When we sit down and start throwing ideas back and forth, one inspires the other and triggers new thoughts, new directions. That process brings about a type of thinking Leo and I could not achieve if we were working separately."

Sharing and cooperation were not always the case for Leo and Diane. When they first met as art students in New York City, they were both impressed by the other's work, but each also felt somewhat threatened by the other's talent.

"It was years and years before we could pass a piece of work back and forth between us and not get into a fight."

"It wasn't merely a matter of competition," Leo recalls, "it was war. We spent a lot of time and energy trying to prove ourselves to each other. In the midst of all that, we fell in love."

After their marriage Leo and Diane decided to work as an illustrating team. Diane explains, "The competition between us was still so strong that we knew we would never survive separate careers. We felt that working as a team would probably help keep our marriage together."

Leo believes that the key to their success was developing a

technique that allows them to share the creative process. "It is important," he says, "that we work on the same piece of art in such a way that nobody knows who did what. After years and years of collaboration, we have reached a point where our work is done by an agent we call *the third artist*." The mysterious third artist, according to Leo and Diane, is a combination of their talents, feelings, and ideas.

Working together isn't always easy. Occasionally there are small arguments. "Sometimes we do disagree," Diane admits. "We argue over things and get mad at each other, but that's life!"

After years of sharing the same studio, Diane and Leo now work in separate studios in their brownstone home. Leo confesses that sharing a studio was sometimes difficult. "I tend to like to play the music loud, and Diane doesn't like that. I also have a habit of playing a song, if I like it, about 40 times in a row. I just keep playing it over and over. It's wonderful!"

Laughing, Diane chimes in, "It can drive you crazy too."

A Wealth of Possibilities

After Leo and Diane read a manuscript and decide they want to illustrate it, they select a style and technique that will work best for the book. One day a particularly strong manuscript arrived at their home, Verna Aardema's *Why Mosquitoes Buzz in People's Ears*. "When we first read the manuscript," Diane recalls, "we were both amazed that in just a few pages there was such a wealth of material. We were quite delighted with all the visual possibilities."

This splendid story brought forth some of the Dillons' most original work. Diane said, "Our real feeling about aiming for perfection began with *Mosquitoes*. Suddenly it seemed that neither of us could tolerate even a tiny flaw—a minute speck on the black night sky. We strove for artistic perfection on that book more than on any other before it."

The Dillons do much more than illustrate words. Through their art, they enrich the text by adding small touches, new layers of meaning. In 1976 they were awarded the Caldecott Medal for *Mosquitoes*. Diane recalled, "In a way, when *Mosquitoes* won the Caldecott Medal, it was as much a reward for us as an award. We had worked harder to achieve perfection—although, of course, we didn't achieve it—than we ever had before, and people somehow knew it."

DO IT YOURSELF!

The Dillons work as a team. As a result, their illustrations have a richness and beauty that could not be achieved if the two artists worked independently. To appreciate their creative process, try working on an art project with a partner. Like Leo and Diane, you'll have to discuss the project before deciding which materials to use. You'll also have to learn how to trust and respect each other's abilities.

Lois Ehlert

Born: November 9, 1934, in Beaver Dam, Wisconsin
Home: Milwaukee, Wisconsin

SELECTED TITLES

Growing Vegetable Soup
1987

Planting a Rainbow
1988

Chicka Chicka Boom Boom
1989

Color Zoo
(Caldecott Honor Book)
1989

Eating the Alphabet
1989

Feathers for Lunch
1990

Red Leaf, Yellow Leaf
1991

Circus
1992

Cuckoo: A Mexican Folktale
1997

Hands
1997

Top Cat
1998

Market Day
2000

Colorful, bright, bold, stunning—these are some of the words that describe Lois Ehlert's artwork. One book reviewer even called it "eye-zapping"! Whatever words we find to describe Lois's books, each page shows the handiwork of a true artist.

"I just love color," Lois affirms. "It makes me happy!" It's true: There is a joyfulness in her books—a sense of wonder, playfulness, startling beauty. A lover of long walks and open spaces, Lois strives to connect her readers to the natural world of gardens and trees, flowers and animals. Lois admits, "I'm trying to use my art to teach a little—making children a little more appreciative of the flowers they can see, or helping to open up their eyes to the beautiful birds flying overhead.

"I guess everyone is influenced by his or her own experiences," Lois says. "Being creative was most natural to me as I was growing up. My mother sewed and my dad built things out of wood. Dad had a workshop in the basement; Mom had a room with all of her material, thread, patterns, and sewing machine. I got good scraps from both of them. They didn't think it was unusual for me to be making things, because that's what they did."

> ### "I think I was born with certain ideas and feelings just waiting to burst out."

In a house where everybody was busy making things, it was only natural that Lois would create art of her own. As a child Lois also loved going to the library with her younger brother and sister. It was a joyous time. "We would go to the library once a week. The maximum number of books we could take out was five per person. We ended up with 15 books each week. We'd take those home, and the three of us would read all 15 one way or another.

We'd take them back and next week get 15 new ones!"

Lois went on to art school, which she enjoyed very much. She discovered that she didn't like drawing as much as she liked cutting and pasting. She describes the thinking behind this preference: "Unless I used a lot of erasers and kept changing the drawing, it never was exactly the way I wanted it. For instance, if I drew a face, I would never know whether the mouth would look better one inch closer to the nose unless I did the drawing over and over again. But if I cut out a mouth of paper, I could try it in different positions until I found the best one, then glue it down permanently."

This art technique, called collage, gave Lois the flexibility she sought. She delights in making pictures out of "found" material—scraps of paper, pieces of fabric, and so on. What's more, it connects Lois to her own childhood days, using materials that her parents left behind.

"I'm just like my dad," Lois admits. "I save all sorts of things—scraps of leather, shiny buttons, colored ribbons, telephone wire. All of this stuff is stored in an old wooden seed box, waiting for a place in my artwork."

Most times Lois writes and illustrates her own books. But when an editor sends her a manuscript written by someone else, Lois will sometimes agree to provide illustrations. One day Lois received a manuscript by Bill Martin, Jr. called *Chicka Chicka Boom Boom*. She almost turned it down!

Lois recalls, "The first time I read it, I thought, This is one I'm not going to be able to do. There's no way. I'll just have to send this back to the editor. Then I started thinking about it, reading the text over again. It has such a nice rhythm, I got to thinking about it almost as a piece of music. I thought, Well, I can maybe just sort of make it like a fiesta."

Lois went right to work: cutting, pasting, painting. Slowly her ideas started to take shape. Lois recalls the process: "I added the borders on the outside and started cutting paper and seeing how I could *possibly* get a letter of the alphabet to climb up a coconut tree!"

Feathers for Lunch

Lois Ehlert

DO IT YOURSELF!

Lois Ehlert believes that every artist needs his or her own space—a special place where he or she can be left alone to create. She offers this advice: "Find a spot where you live— it can be small—to keep all the supplies you might need when you write or draw. When an idea comes, you'll be ready. Good luck to you. I know I can always use a bit of luck myself!"

Mem Fox

Born: March 5, 1946, in Melbourne, Australia
Home: Adelaide, Australia

SELECTED TITLES

Possum Magic
1983

Wilfrid Gordon McDonald Partridge
1984

Hattie and the Fox
1986

Koala Lou
1988

Night Noises
1989

Shoes From Grandpa
1990

Dear Mem Fox, I Have Read All Your Books Even the Pathetic Ones
1992

Time for Bed
1993

Whoever You Are
1997

Sleepy Bears
1999

Harriet, You'll Drive Me Wild!
2000

Mem Fox is a woman of great enthusiasm. When talking, Mem will often hoot with delight and flail her arms to make a point. Or she'll lean forward, listening intently, her eyes fixed and steady. And always, at a moment's notice Mem is ready to fill a room with uproarious laughter.

Naturally, this emotional zest spills over into Mem's writing. Mem believes that, above all, a book should make the reader *feel*. "Emotion is to picture books as flour is to bread," Mem contends. "If we don't laugh, gasp, block our ears, sigh, vomit, giggle, curl our toes, sympathize, feel pain, weep, or shiver during the reading of a picture book, then surely the writer has wasted our time, our money, and our precious trees."

Born in Melbourne, Australia, Mem moved to Africa with her parents, who were missionaries, when she was only six months old. They lived in Rhodesia, now called Zimbabwe. Mem loved her first school and made many friends. She recalls, "I spoke the local language, Ndebele, better than I spoke English. Like the other children in my class, I learned to write by writing letters with my finger, in the dusty, red earth."

Finally Published

While growing up, Mem made occasional stabs at writing. Laughing at the recollection, she confides that her first book, written at age ten, "was about the thrilling subject of soil erosion." However, the world of theater also tugged at Mem's heart. At age 19 Mem moved to London to study drama, but after a few years she decided that she preferred writing to acting. Back in Australia, now with a husband, Malcolm, and a child, Chloe, Mem began to work on a story called *Hush, the Invisible Mouse*. Mem remembers the motivation behind writing the story: "It came about because I was enraged that my daughter had no books to help her identify herself as an Australian, to help her feel proud of her country and her heritage." So Mem wrote the story of Hush, and lovingly wrapped it in the texture and details of Australian life.

Mem tried to get her picture book published, but no one seemed interested in her story. Mem recalls: "Each time I received a rejection slip, I felt ashamed that I'd dared to believe the book might be worth publishing."

But with the unfailing support of her husband, Mem persevered. She rewrote her story 23 times. Finally, one quiet day in Australia, the air was pierced with Mem's whoops of joy. After five years and nine rejections, a publisher wanted to publish her book. "I was wild with excitement," Mem remembers. "I changed the mouse to a possum and called the story *Possum Magic*. The irony," Mem adds with obvious satisfaction, "is that *Possum Magic* became the best-selling children's book in the history of Australia."

Of all the books she has written, Mem's favorite is *Koala Lou*. This may be because the central character in the story—an earnest little koala who desperately wants to succeed and be loved—is really Mem. Mem explains, "*Koala Lou* is about me and my mum, who's really tough. She is a female Tarzan, the kind of person who will kill a snake with a crowbar without flinching. She loves me a lot but she never says 'I love you.' Never."

When writing, Mem needs solitude, silence, and a clean work space. Getting the initial idea is the first and hardest part (though, Mem insists, there are *many* hard parts). Mem explains, "I always write in pencil first so that I can rub out as I go."

She confides, "The ideas leap into my head from real life, and if they don't, I don't write. I'm not one of those disciplined writers who sits down at a blank piece of paper or a blank computer screen and says, 'I'm not moving until I've written five hundred words.' I could sit there for a month without writing a word."

A fierce perfectionist, Mem actually spends most of her writing time rewriting. She recalls: "It took me two years to write *Koala Lou*, even though it's only 410 words. I did 49 drafts for *Koala Lou* before the book was ready to be published."

KOALA LOU

WRITTEN BY **Mem Fox**   ILLUSTRATED BY **Pamela Lofts**

DO IT YOURSELF!

Mem's books are loaded with action and good dialogue. She strives to reveal characters by what they do and say rather than by describing them. That's why it's fun to put on a play based on her books. *Wilfrid Gordon McDonald Partridge* is a great place to start, but use any book you like. You'll have to get some classmates to help out. On with the show!

Gail Gibbons

Born: August 1, 1944, in Oak Park, Illinois
Home: Corinth, Vermont

A strong-willed, independent child, Gail Gibbons used to drive adults a little crazy. "I drove my parents nuts," she admits with a laugh. "And I drove my teachers nuts, too, because I wouldn't fit into their ideas of what kids were supposed to do. I was usually in the last seat in the row because the teacher couldn't see what I was doing back there. I wanted to be drawing and sketching and doing other things."

Gail wasn't the kind of child who settled for a simple answer, either. Even as a child she had a thirst to understand things. It was never enough for Gail to know what time it was, she had to know how the whole clock worked! That's probably why Gail writes nonfiction books today. She thinks the world is full of all sorts of "neat, interesting stuff." Gail loves learning new things and explaining them through words and pictures to young readers.

Gail began her career by working in television. She used to work as a graphic artist on *The Today Show, Saturday Night Live,* and a children's show, *Take a Giant Step.* Gail remembers, "That's when the interest in children's books began . . . so I started writing and illustrating for children."

"I like to come away from reading a book with the feeling that I've learned something. That's why I like nonfiction."

Encouraged by her husband, Kent, Gail decided to try her hand at nonfiction books. At that time most nonfiction books were drab and dull. Almost none had colorful illustrations. Gail felt that she could use the techniques she had learned in television graphics to make nonfiction books that were bright and alive. Gail explains, "With television graphics, you're lucky if the piece you design is on the screen for six seconds. So I had learned how to make art that's simplified and easily readable. It has to be something that grabs you—not

cluttered and fancy. When I'm doing a book, it's pretty much the same thing. I love working with bright, bold, beautiful colors."

From the Beginning

Gail begins each book by selecting a topic, usually with the help of an editor. It's important that they both agree. She says, "This morning an editor called and asked if I wanted to do a couple of sports books. Well I don't like sports, so I don't want to do that. It has to be something that I'm interested in." Once they agree on a topic, Gail moves on to the next stage: research.

"I go to bookstores and libraries to gather information, but I don't trust books solely, because they can have mistakes. So I find an expert, someone who knows a lot about the subject I'm writing about. That way I'm sure to get the most up-to-date information."

Gail admits, "I always end up with much more information than I can use. I want to make absolutely sure I've covered everything. If you notice, in many of my books there's a lot of information on page 32. Those are extra things that I found that I think are sort of neat, except I couldn't fit them elsewhere in the book."

Next comes perhaps the most important stage of all. Gail begins the painstaking process of selecting the most important facts and organizing them into a clear structure. In an approach similar to the way she draws pictures, Gail tries to simplify the information, deciding which details are essential and which only make it more complicated. She is always asking herself, "What's the most important thing?"

A mother of two children, Becky and Eric, Gail believes it's important to keep in touch with her readers. She travels about seven weeks a year, going from classroom to classroom. Letters from readers also help Gail find out what children really think about her books. She describes her most memorable letter: "The best letter I ever got went like this: 'Dear Gail, I love your books. Right now I am—oh there's a spider crawling across the page! SQUASH.'" Gail laughs and says, "There was a dead spider squashed right on the letter. It was hysterical. I saved that letter. And I still have the dead spider!"

DO IT YOURSELF!

Like Gail Gibbons, start by selecting a topic to write about. Then go to the library and begin your research. You may want to find an expert to help you. Decide which facts are most fun and important. And remember Gail's tip: "Write about something you know about. Write about what you like. You'll enjoy it a lot more!"

Patricia Reilly Giff

Born: April 26, 1935, in Brooklyn, New York
Home: Weston, Connecticut

SELECTED TITLES

Fourth-Grade Celebrity
1979

Today Was a Terrible Day
1980

Have You Seen Hyacinth Macaw?
1981

The Winter Worm Business
1981

Gift of the Pirate Queen
1982

The Almost Awful Play
1984

Watch Out, Ronald Morgan!
1985

Matthew Jackson Meets the Wall
1990

Lily's Crossing
(Newbery Honor Book)
1997

Nory Ryan's Song
2000

"Anybody can write a book," states Patricia Reilly Giff, the author behind several popular book series (including The Polk Street Kids). "I mean, look at me. Over 70 books and not one bit of talent! I know it sounds funny, but I really do believe it. Writing is something you have to learn. It is a craft. It takes practice. If you set your mind to something, no matter how hard it is, you can do it. That's my message to kids: Go for it. If you want something in life, work at it and you can get it."

Patricia (Pat to her friends) sees herself as living proof that an ordinary person can become a successful writer. She stresses, "I don't think writing is a gift. We learn to speak, we learn to read, we learn to write. Writing is a natural thing, not a special talent. Writing is something you learn, because you do it all the time."

A Late Bloomer

Pat's career did not come easy. Ever since she was a child, Pat wanted to be a writer. But as she grew older, she became nervous about sharing her work with others. Pat confesses, "I didn't write until I was grown up because I didn't think I was good enough. I was afraid people might laugh at me."

It wasn't until she was 40 that Pat made a brave decision. She would write a story—even, she says, if it took the rest of her life. "I decided that I would write every day for a year," Pat explains. Working full-time as a teacher, Pat would drag herself out of bed in the early morning to write for an hour. Pat recalls, "Slowly and painfully, I began to form the words, the sentences. And then suddenly writing became one of the most important parts of my life, a part that now I couldn't do without."

Today Patricia Reilly Giff is praised as a writer who truly

understands children. When she writes dialogue, it crackles with energy. When she describes a classroom scene, it springs vividly to life. And it should—Pat has spent plenty of time in schools, first as a classroom teacher and then as a reading specialist.

> ### "I try to write books that say ordinary people are special."

Pat says, "I wanted to write about kids. I wanted to write about their world. The cafeteria, what goes on during holidays, climbing the ropes in gym—all those things had happened again and again in my life. After I started working on the Polk Street series, school life really began to come alive in my writing."

Pat draws upon real people as a basis for her characters. She thinks of the children she knew in school, her own three children, and the feelings she herself had as a child. Pat identifies with the underdog; she has a soft spot for the child who isn't perfect. She likes kids who don't always hit home runs, who don't always get 100s on tests. Pat advises, "You never want to write about a perfect person. Look at Ramona Quimby. She's not perfect, but it's the failings that remind us of ourselves. That's what builds a character."

Pat loves to listen to kids talk. It helps her write dialogue. "Writing dialogue is my strength," she says. "I almost hate to say that, because serious readers may not think it's important. But for me, dialogue is the most wonderful part of writing. I can remember exact conversations from 25 years ago. I can remember the sound of a person's voice."

Throughout Pat's life, from childhood to adulthood, at work and at play, books have always been close by. Cherished objects, books have played a central role in her world. Pat remembers, "As a child, I read in bed before the sun was up, then hunched over the breakfast table with a book in my lap. After school I'd sit in the kitchen, leaning against the warm radiator, dreaming over a story. My mother would say, 'Go out and play, go out and play.' I hated to go out and play! All I wanted to do was dream over stories."

DO IT YOURSELF!

How do people talk? If you're writing dialogue, it's an important question. Patricia Reilly Giff listens carefully when people speak. She has noticed, for example, that people rarely finish their sentences. Think of two people you know very well—two friends, perhaps—and write down a conversation they might have. Try to make it as realistic as possible!

Phoebe Gilman

Born: April 4, 1940, in New York, New York
Home: Toronto, Ontario, Canada

SELECTED TITLES

The Balloon Tree
1984

Jillian Jiggs
(first in a series)
1985

*The Wonderful Pigs
of Jillian Jiggs*
1989

*Grandma and
the Pirates*
1990

*Once Upon a
Golden Apple*
1991

Something From Nothing
1992

The Gypsy Princess
1995

Phoebe Gilman doesn't get ideas—the ideas get her. Phoebe says, "You get obsessed with this kernel of an idea, and no matter how hard you try to ignore it, it keeps working away at you."

That initial idea may be a passing comment she overhears, something funny she sees, or a thought that floats through her mind. But once the idea grabs hold, there's no letting go. "Some of my books are very easy to write," Phoebe says. "Others just go on and on until I think, Oh, am I ever going to do anything with this idea or is it going to torture me forever?"

The Balloon Tree is a good example. Phoebe says that she had the basic idea for more than ten years. But ideas alone are not books. "The idea is just the beginning," Phoebe explains. "What's important is the determination to sit down and work at it. But without an idea, you're nowhere."

Phoebe admits there are times when the ideas simply don't come. She says, "I've learned that there are times when I just have to run away from my ideas. I often think of the *Sesame Street* character who composes songs on the piano. Instead of 'Mary had a little lamb' he'll sing, 'Mary had a little dog.' Then he gets frustrated, bangs his head on the piano, and cries, 'I'll *never* get it right.' I identify with that feeling completely."

> **"My experience is that when you sit down to think of an idea for a new book, your mind goes blank. So it's very handy to scribble ideas down right away. Otherwise they evaporate."**

Though she tries to avoid it, Phoebe does bang her head on the piano a few times before she's satisfied with a book. "It's like

with *Grandma and the Pirates*," Phoebe recalls. "The story started out as 'Grandma's Chocolate Chicken.' It went through so many drafts. But I've learned to tell myself, Okay, calm down. I guess you're just going to have to go shopping." But, she admits with a devious chuckle, "It can get expensive!"

At the beginning of the writing process, Phoebe—who both writes and illustrates her books—will write down whatever pops into her head, without worrying whether it's good. Phoebe describes the process: "I write very freely at first, just tons of stuff. At that stage, I try not to revise at all. If the editor in my head comes in too soon and says, Ugh, this isn't good, then nothing ever gets past the early stages."

A Thousand and One Hats

Afterward, when Phoebe sits back and reads her first draft, she switches roles from writer to editor. Phoebe deletes words, crosses out paragraphs, throws entire pages away. Finally, when Phoebe Gilman the editor is satisfied, Phoebe Gilman the illustrator steps in.

She confesses, "I must have a thousand and one hats like Dr. Seuss's Bartholomew Cubbins, because when my editor's hat comes off, I have to put on my

illustrator's hat. I have to look at the story and say to myself, *Arrgh*, how am I going to draw this? I don't know how to draw horses. I grew up in the Bronx."

Phoebe often likes to use

models for her pictures. Using models, she believes, helps keep her illustrations from getting stale. "I think if you draw only from your head, then all of your characters begin to look alike. But when you go back to drawing real people, you start to notice things. You say, Oh, my goodness, look at the weird shape of his ears."

When the book is finally completed, Phoebe sends it off to the publisher. For her, this creates a feeling of emptiness, as if a good friend just moved away. Phoebe recalls, "You say to yourself, What am I going to play with now?"

And so the process begins once again.

DO IT YOURSELF!

Phoebe Gilman suggests that kids put on a play based on any of the Jillian Jiggs books. She says, "It lends itself to plays, because there's lots of action, costumes, and dialogue. For added fun, stop the action at any point and then improvise what happens next."

Paul Goble

Born: September 27, 1933, in Haslemere, England
Home: Lincoln, Nebraska

SELECTED TITLES

The Girl Who Loved Wild Horses
(Caldecott Medal)
1978

The Gift of the Sacred Dog
1980

Buffalo Woman
1984

Death of the Iron Horse
1987

Iktomi and the Boulder
(first in a series)
1988

Dream Wolf
1990

I Sing for the Animals
1991

Crow Chief: A Plains Indian Story
1992

Adopted by the Eagles
1994

The Return of the Buffaloes
1996

The Legend of the White Buffalo Woman
1998

Paul Goble has been interested in Native American culture for as long as he can remember. He recalls, "One of my early memories is of walking around my suburban neighborhood in England, dressed in my American Indian regalia: fringed shirt, leggings, and war bonnet, all of which my mother had made for me. I remember being absolutely certain that anyone who saw me would think I was a real Indian!"

As a child, Paul longed to visit the land where Native Americans once flourished. When he was 26 years old, Paul finally came to America and witnessed Native American dances and ceremonies. Though exhilarating, the experience left him saddened. Paul saw that many of the Indian children were more interested in baseball than in their own heritage. It gave him a reason to write. He says, "It was primarily with these children in mind that I wrote and illustrated my first books. I wanted them to feel proud of their own culture. It was important that their parents like the books, but it was even more important that their great-grandparents would smile, recognizing in my pictures and stories the proud old days that they knew about."

The Lessons of Myth

In 1977 Paul came to live permanently in the United States, first in South Dakota and later in Nebraska. A year later he won the prestigious Caldecott Medal for *The Girl Who Loved Wild Horses*. It was all the encouragement he needed.

Paul has a great love for the mythology of the Plains Indians. In it he finds many valuable lessons. "I think that most people today understand the word *myth* to mean 'fantasy' but that is exactly the opposite of what it was intended to mean," Paul contends. "All of the world's truths are conveyed in myths. More than just stories, the traditional Indian myths show us how older generations of Indians understood the world."

Sometimes the myths are parables, or stories with moral lessons. Paul's book *Dream Wolf* is a kind of parable. Paul gives his interpretation of the story: "This is

the lesson: The Creator made all things, and so room must be made for all things. We are part of a whole, and wolves too are a part of that whole."

> *"As a child, I took the great Indian leaders of history as my heroes. Football players or pop stars were too ordinary to be my heroes."*

Paul is saddened that modern man has brutally hunted and killed the wolf, driving the animal from its native territory. He contrasts this ruthlessness to the attitude of the Plains Indians, who felt grateful toward all animals because they provided food. They believed all beings on the earth were connected as one. Paul concludes, "Where the wolf no longer roams, he is missed by everything in nature. We feel his loss; creation is incomplete."

In his work, Paul Goble is, by his own admission, a fierce traditionalist. He strives to make every aspect of his books absolutely accurate. Paul says, "I make great efforts to get things right, both in words and pictures. I find it annoying to see illustrators who illustrate Native American scenes without any real knowledge behind what they are drawing." To avoid mistakes, Paul, who has been adopted by the Yakima and Sioux tribes, relies on thorough research. He says, "I am writing and picturing things of more than 100 years ago. I have to know the museums well, and I revisit them again and again."

Yet Paul's research amounts to more than hours spent hunched over ancient tomes in dusty libraries. Much of it is on-site; he often visits Indian reservations and encampments. When Paul writes a story, his goal is to re-create the time when the tale was first told. He wants readers to feel as though they are in a tepee, years ago, with the storyteller seated before a glowing fire.

Paul sees his work as a way of giving back to the Indians the treasures that were already theirs. By bringing a forgotten tale into the light, Paul helps to preserve a great and noble culture. His books offer a glimpse of what Native American life was like back in the buffalo days, when the Plains Indians were at their height. Paul concludes, "I have simply wanted to express and to share these things that I love so much."

THE GIRL WHO LOVED WILD HORSES
by PAUL GOBLE

DO IT YOURSELF!

Paul Goble tries to re-create the mood of an oral telling. Paul says that the storyteller would often add hand gestures and facial expressions to the story. Try it yourself. Read a story again and again until you really understand it. Think of gestures that you can add to make the tale come alive. Then get a circle of friends together . . . and tell them a story!

Eloise Greenfield

Born: May 17, 1929, in Parmele, North Carolina
Home: Washington, D.C.

Eloise Greenfield has always been motivated by a deep love of language. Intricately tied to this love is another even greater motivation. Eloise explains, "There's a desperate need for more black literature for children, for a large body of literature in which black children can see themselves and their lives and history reflected. I want to do my share in building it."

Eloise's books touch on recurring themes of family love and human relationships. She has written biographies about the lives and historical contributions of black Americans such as Rosa Parks and Paul Robeson. Her poetry celebrates the syntax and rhythms of black language and black life. Speaking of her commitment to her work, Eloise says, "It is necessary for black children to have a true knowledge of their past and present, in order that they may develop an informed sense of direction for their future."

Growing Up

Except for three months in Parmele, North Carolina, Eloise Greenfield has spent her entire life in Washington, D.C. She recalls: "When I was three months old,

Daddy left home to make a way for us. He went north, as thousands of black people had done, during slavery and since. They went north looking for safety, for justice, for freedom, for work—for a good life. Often one member of a family would go ahead of the others to make a way—to find a job and a place to live. And that's what my father did."

The second oldest of five children, Eloise looks back on her childhood in Washington, D.C., with fondness. "We didn't have much money, but my father always had a job and we were able to manage . . . . We went to movies and to the Howard Theater, where great jazz musicians like Duke Ellington performed. Both of my parents loved the arts, so we were always doing something."

> **"I want to choose and order words that children will want to celebrate. I want to make them shout and laugh and blink back tears and care about themselves."**

On her ninth birthday, Eloise and her family moved into a new housing project named Langston Terrace. For Eloise, it was love at first sight. She remembers, "It was built on a hill, a group of tan brick houses and apartments with a playground as its center. The red mud surrounding the concrete walks had not yet been covered with black soil and grass seed, and the holes that would soon be homes for young trees were filled with rainwater. But it still looked beautiful to me.

"There were so many games to play and things to do. We played hide-and-seek at the lamppost, paddle tennis and shuffleboard, dodge ball and jacks. We danced in fireplug showers; jumped rope to rhymes; played Bouncy Bouncy Bally, swinging one leg over a bouncing ball; played baseball on a nearby field; had parties in the social room and bus trips to the beach."

Although childhood was a magical time, it was also touched by racism. "There were a lot of things we couldn't do and places we couldn't go. Washington was a city for white people. But inside that city, there was another city. It didn't have a name and it wasn't all in one area, but it was where black people lived."

Eloise admits that writing was "the farthest thing from my mind when I was growing up. I loved words, but I loved to *read* them, not write them." While working at the U.S. Patent Office, though, Eloise got started writing. In 1963 she published her first poem. But she did not begin to write for children until after meeting Sharon Bell Mathis, a fellow member of the D.C. Black Writers Workshop.

Eloise says, "Sharon talked so passionately about the need for good black books that it was contagious. Once I realized the full extent of the problem, it became urgent for me to try, along with others, to build a large collection of books for children."

Eloise Greenfield is a major voice in children's literature. Her books celebrate the strength within each of us to overcome obstacles, the need for family togetherness in difficult times, and the transcendent power of language itself.

DO IT YOURSELF!

Eloise has written biographies of people whom she admires. She says, "I enjoyed doing them. The research is always interesting. I selected them because I felt they were people children needed to meet." Whom do you admire? Write a brief biography of someone (it could be a famous person or a kind neighbor who lives down the street). Think of it as a way of introducing two friends: "Here's someone you should know!"

Ruth Heller

Born: April 2, 1924, in Winnipeg, Manitoba, Canada
Home: San Francisco, California

SELECTED TITLES

Chickens Aren't the Only Ones
1981

Animals Born Alive and Well
1982

The Reason for a Flower
1983

Plants That Never Ever Bloom
1984

A Cache of Jewels: And Other Collective Nouns
1987

Kites Sail High: A Book About Verbs
1988

Many Luscious Lollipops: A Book About Adjectives
1989

Merry-Go-Round: A Book About Nouns
1990

Up, Up and Away: A Book About Adverbs
1991

Fantastic! Wow! and Unreal!: A Book About Interjections and Conjunctions
1998

"Galápagos" Means "Tortoises"
2000

"**I**'ve been interested in art for as long as I can remember," Ruth Heller says with characteristic gusto. "I've always loved coloring and cutting and pasting and drawing—and generally making a big mess."

Growing up, Ruth remembers copying comic strips from the newspaper. In school she would always add a picture or two to her reports. She says, "I loved school. But it wasn't until the upper grades that I was able to study art."

After completing school, Ruth went on to become a designer and illustrator. She did all sorts of interesting work. Ruth recalls, "I began my career designing wrapping paper, cocktail napkins, kites, mugs, greeting cards, posters, and then coloring books." One day a visit to an aquarium triggered an idea. She decided to try her hand at writing.

Ruth recalls the day: "While researching at Steinhart Aquarium for a coloring book on tropical fish, I became intrigued with a strange-looking shape floating in one of the tanks and found that it was the egg sac of a dogfish shark. This led me to read about other egg-laying animals. My reading stimulated visions of colors and shapes and compositions. In addition to this visual wealth, I had found enough information to convince me that I wanted to write and illustrate a book."

Creating the book was easy compared to trying to sell it to a publisher. "It took me five years to get it published," Ruth says. "I contacted the most prestigious publishers in the world—and I have rejections from all of them!"

Part of the problem was that Ruth's style was so different from what people were used to seeing. At that time, in the mid-1970s, most nonfiction books for children were painfully boring. Then along came Ruth Heller with an entirely different approach. She not only used bright, beautiful illustrations but also wrote in rhyme! Ruth remembers, "Editors didn't know

what to do with the book. I was told that children who'd enjoy the pictures were too young for the information. And that students who would be able to understand the vocabulary would find a picture book too babyish."

"I've done five books on parts of speech. A lot of people think that's a pretty dry subject. Doing it in rhyme, with colorful illustrations, helps bring it to life."

Luckily, one editor took a chance and published *Chickens Aren't the Only Ones*. Today, thanks to Ruth Heller and other innovative writers such as Joanna Cole, Gail Gibbons, and Kate Waters, children can read nonfiction books that are every bit as lively and imaginative as favorite storybooks.

Keeping It Fresh

"I try to make every page a complete surprise," Ruth says of her work. "I make a tremendous effort not to repeat myself." To get started, she needs to look at pictures of her subject. Ruth says, "I do everything. I go to the zoo and take pictures. I buy loads and loads of books and magazines. I keep a file of photographs I think

I might need someday. I'm not good at imagining. I have to have either the actual object or a photograph in front of me."

Sometimes Ruth works so hard she can't stop thinking about the book she's writing. She reveals, "I'm constantly thinking of the words and the rhymes. I'll fall asleep at night with the words swirling in my head and wake up in the morning and hopefully the words are still there."

Ruth offers this advice to young writers: "I think it's terribly important to read as much as you can. I don't think you can get much out of your head unless you put things into it. I also think it's very important to keep a journal. As with a diary, start with what you did that day. From there on, you'll find that the writing itself will open up all sorts of thoughts and feelings."

Fantastic! Wow! And Unreal!
A Book About Interjections and Conjunctions
BY RUTH HELLER

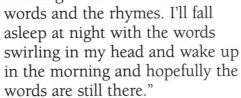

DO IT YOURSELF!

Ruth Heller finds writing in rhyme to be both challenging and fun. The challenge for Ruth is that her rhymes have to convey facts. Try it yourself. First, write down some simple directions, such as how to get to your house from school. Then try to get across the same information—but in rhyme. As Ruth might tell you, it may not be easy, but it sure will be fun!

Kevin Henkes

Born: November 27, 1960, in Racine, Wisconsin
Home: Madison, Wisconsin

SELECTED TITLES

All Alone
1981

A Weekend With Wendell
1986

Sheila Rae, the Brave
1987

Chester's Way
1988

Jessica
1989

Julius, the Baby of the World
1990

Chrysanthemum
1991

Owen
(Caldecott Honor Book)
1993

Lilly's Purple Plastic Purse
1996

Wemberly Worried
2000

For writers, the creative process differs with the demands of each book. Few can point to a map and say, "This is exactly how I get there, every time." But despite the differences, patterns do emerge. For Kevin Henkes (HENG-kiss), the genesis of a book often begins with a character. The storyline then naturally flows out of that character; in other words, story can be seen as a revelation of character.

Kevin explains, "I almost always have the character first. The only way a book can be real, for me, is to have the character first and then take the story from there."

This should come as no surprise to Kevin's fans. For nearly 20 years (about half his life!), Kevin Henkes has created a long list of endearing characters and enduring books. There's Lilly and Sheila Rae, Wemberly and Chester, Owen and Chrysanthemum. In fact, the very titles themselves illustrate Kevin's "character first" approach. The stories are quiet and warm, funny and perceptive, and offer a calm, realistic portrayal of children's lives.

Still, it's not as if fully formed characters come knocking on Kevin's door, ready to appear in books. Developing a character,

Kevin says, is a process of discovery. He compares it to taking a photograph, slowly bringing the image into sharper focus. He says, "When I am first thinking about characters, they are kind of cloudy. As I think about them—and maybe as I come to love them—little by little they come into focus."

He points out, "I think what brings them into focus is their particulars. For example, with Wemberly, I wanted it to be a kid who worried. That's fine and good, but when it started working was when I decided that she would have a spot over one eye, and one ear would be spotted—when I decided that she would have some kind of object that she loved and carried around with her. There has to be emotional truth," Kevin says, "but also physical details that are sharp and that's what makes the character unique."

> **"Just because I'm a published author doesn't mean that I don't make lots and lots of mistakes. It doesn't just happen naturally, even if you are good at something. It's hard work."**

Kevin continues, "I don't mention in *Chester's Way* that Lilly wears boots or a crown or a cape. But those were the details that came to me before I had put words on the page. Those were the things that made me want to write about her. It's those details that make a character interesting."

One reason Kevin's characters appear so complete is that he realizes that characters must have depth. And in order to have depth, a character must have both strengths and flaws. "If a character is not fully developed," Kevin offers, "then that character will be flat and dull. That's why, in *Sheila Rae, the Brave*, she was brave . . . but she wasn't. And her sister Louise was not brave . . . but she was. I remember wanting to show Sheila Rae cry. I thought that helped make her a more believable, well-rounded character."

As a child, Kevin was always drawing. He recalls, "I knew I would be an artist." Along with his passion for art, Kevin also loved to write. Picture books, he discovered early on, allowed him to combine those two talents.

"It's always the story that comes first," Kevin claims. "You can be the world's best painter, but you may not be able to create a picture book. Today so many picture books are just decorative. But the art form of the picture book is, in fact, all 32 pages—pictures and words—working together."

"I'll write the story, and that can take anywhere from a week to two months. When I write a picture book, I don't like to force anything. I write three lines, and that may take three hours. But I'll sit there and just doodle if I have to. Usually I'll have the opening and I'll know where I want to end up; working on the middle takes the most time."

Kevin muses, "When I was young, I thought that if a person was going to be an author, then he or she needed to have done extraordinary things, traveled around the word and had great adventures. But if you're a writer, then . . . you're a writer. No matter how humble your life may be, we all have stories to tell."

DO IT YOURSELF!

To Kevin's surprise, he's found that certain characters—Lilly, most insistently—stay with him long after he's completed "their" book. It's almost as if they tug on his sleeve, saying "Write another story about me!" Kevin almost has no choice but to oblige. Try it yourself. Read *Chester's Way* and *Lilly's Purple Plastic Purse*. Then try to write a new story about Lilly—perhaps even using something from your own life for inspiration.

Gloria Houston

Born: November 24, year unavailable, in Marion, North Carolina
Home: Tamoa, Florida

SELECTED TITLES

My Brother Joey Died
1982

The Year of the Perfect
Christmas Tree: An
Appalachian Story
1988

Littlejim
1990

But No Candy
1992

My Great-Aunt Arizona
1992

Littlejim's Gift
1994

Mountain Valor
1994

Bright Freedom's Song:
A Story of the
Underground Railroad
1998

Gloria Houston grew up in a small town nestled in the forbidding beauty of the Appalachian Mountains. It was a simple, rural way of life—full of colorful characters and strong traditions. Her family still runs the country store where she grew up listening to people come and go, swapping stories of everyday events. But it was at home that Gloria was most "steeped in storytelling." Her father and mother loved to tell stories about the family and local history, and it is these tales that have most influenced Gloria's work.

"Many of my books so far have been based on characters and incidents from Avery County, North Carolina, my childhood home," says Gloria. "*My Great-Aunt Arizona* is about my fourth-grade teacher, and it's all true. *The Year of the Perfect Christmas Tree*, on the other hand, is all fiction, though I based it on people I know. I wrote it as a Christmas gift to my mother."

Sharing Family Stories

Gloria is proud of her Appalachian homeland. "One of my goals as a writer is to help my young readers become acquainted with its wonderful culture.

"I always knew I would be a writer," she reveals. "When I was seven, my Aunt Wilma gave me a copy of *Little Women*. In that book I found a kindred soul, Jo, and I knew that I would grow up to be like she was."

Nevertheless, it is one thing to be a writer and quite another to be a published writer. It took Gloria years of rejection before one of her books was accepted for publication. She remembers, "*My Brother Joey Died* had 54 rejections. I still have them all in a file. It became like a game, 'Well, let's see how many more I can collect!'"

It was a heartbreaking time for the aspiring author. "Rejection was very difficult," Gloria admits. "Trying to get published was in part an

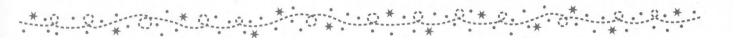

attempt to build my self-esteem. What a way to build it—with 54 rejections! One way I dealt with it was to keep telling people that I was a writer. I told everybody who would listen: 'I'm a writer, I'm a writer, I'm going to be a writer.' And I wrote my little head off while I was saying it. I was trying to convince everybody else while I was convincing myself."

"I think that the stories within our families are an important part of who we are and give us a sense of belonging that few other things do."

Gloria believes that all families have meaningful stories to share. She tells a story to make her point: "Right at this moment, I'm sitting on land that my great-great-great-great-great-grandfather, William Wiseman, got in a land grant from King George III of England. This land has been in my family for seven generations. If it weren't for the hill that's just to my right, I could see William Wiseman's grave. He was a stowaway on a ship from London at age 13. My family has lived in this valley for that long. The oral stories that have been handed down in my family are no different from the oral stories in other families. It's just that we have the tradition of keeping them

alive by telling them."
Readers of Gloria Houston's remarkable books will also come to know another important influence on her life—her great-aunt Arizona. Gloria, who like her great-aunt before her is a teacher, says, "Arizona was a remarkable woman and probably the greatest influence on my life. She truly lives on in what she gave to her students, including me. She spent her entire life teaching within five miles of her birthplace. And yet she has influenced the world through her students."

If there is a message in Gloria's writing, it may be that we should all value our own families, our own cultures, our own stories. Gloria loves to hear from young students who have asked their own parents to tell family stories. Gloria says with satisfaction, "Kids begin to look at their heritages. They begin to think, 'Hey, my family is special!' They begin to talk to their parents and their parents begin to talk to them. They come back with stories that no one ever thought to tell them."

DO IT YOURSELF!

It might be fun to listen to and write down some of your own family stories. But Gloria admits that people aren't always ready to tell a story. They might not even know they have a story to tell. So she offers this tip: "Here are a few specific questions to ask parents: What can you tell me about my grandmother? Where is my grandmother from? What did my grandmother do? These kinds of little questions will prompt stories—and stories are in every family."

Pat Hutchins

Born: June 18, 1942, in Yorkshire, England
Home: London, England

SELECTED TITLES

Rosie's Walk
1968

Good Night, Owl!
1972

The Wind Blew
1974

Happy Birthday, Sam
1978

I Hunter
1982

You'll Soon Grow Into Them, Titch
1983

The Very Worst Monster
1985

The Doorbell Rang
1986

Little Pink Pig
1994

Shrinking Mouse
1997

It's My Birthday!
1999

Ten Red Apples
2000

Pat Hutchins's very first book, *Rosie's Walk*, is a widely loved classic. But without the help of a great editor, the book might never have been published.

Rosie's Walk, a story that uses only 32 words, was once quite different from its final version. "It started off much longer," Pat recalls. "I wrote this extremely boring story that went on forever about animal noises. I remember my editor, Susan Hirschman, reading it. There was one line that said, *This is the fox. He never makes a noise.* Out of all my reams and reams of pages, she said, 'I like that line.'"

With that advice, Pat Hutchins returned home, determined to revise the manuscript. Pat says, "I took her quite literally: The fox doesn't make a noise. So I began to look at the book as if it were a silent film. The audience is aware of what's going on, but the heroine, Rosie, is totally unaware. I think that makes it more exciting, because the reader is in on the joke from the very beginning. The reader has secret knowledge.

"I deliberately designed the book so that the reader, turning the page, is responsible for all the fox's terrible mishaps. I like to think that readers feel very involved in the book: Their action of turning the page creates the action of the story."

Old Sneakers and Pictures

The sixth of seven children, Pat grew up in Yorkshire, England. As a child she often copied pictures from magazines. Pat has a fond memory of an elderly couple, Mr. and Mrs. Bruce, who encouraged her talent. "If I did a particularly good drawing," Pat recalls, "they would reward me with a bar of chocolate."

When Pat completes a book, she says, "It's always with a big sigh of relief. I love the writing, but I do find drawing very, very difficult. I'm usually amazed that I've actually managed to finish the drawings." Soon another feeling creeps in: self-doubt. "Each time I finish a book, I think, That's it, I'll

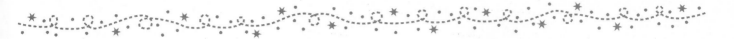

never ever have another idea again! I get quite desperate."

Pat gets ideas from a variety of sources, mostly from observing her children or remembering feelings from her own childhood. She says, "There's no magic formula for coming up with ideas. You've got to try to write about what you know or what you care about. Because generally, if you enjoy something, then there's a good chance that the person reading it will enjoy it as well."

"I think if I drew from now until doomsday, I would never be completely happy with my drawings."

Pat begins each book the same way. "I always start with the words," she says. "I think of myself as a writer first. You can have a beautifully illustrated book, but if it has a terrible story then you can't get away with it."

Pat works in a tiny studio in her London home. She admits, "It's extremely untidy, very messy. It's full of odd things, because I need lots of things for reference. There could be anything in here: old boots, broken old toys, all sorts of junk."

Why all the clutter? Pat offers this explanation: "I'm not very good, for example, at drawing shoes. I don't think I can draw a shoe from memory, so I have a pair of old sneakers in my workroom, just so I can have a look at them, to remind myself what sneakers look like."

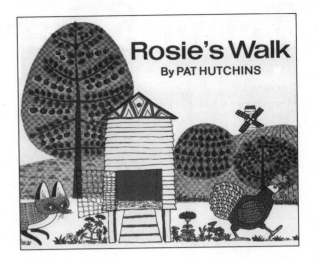

Writing books for children keeps Pat Hutchins on her toes. Though she is always very careful with research, mistakes can happen. And when one does, a smart reader will point it out to her.

Pat recalls one such incident: "The whole crux of *The Mona-Lisa Mystery* is that the *Mona Lisa* is stolen, wrapped around someone's leg, and then covered in a bandage—that's how they escape from the museum with it. One day a child wrote to me and said, 'I enjoyed your book very much, but there's one enormous mistake in it. The *Mona Lisa* is painted on wood, no way could it be wrapped around someone's leg!' So I checked with an art historian, and sure enough, it's painted on wood. It served me right."

DO IT YOURSELF!

In creating a story, a writer is often a problem-solver. For example, in *The Mona-Lisa Mystery*, Pat Hutchins had to figure out a way to steal the painting. Unfortunately, her idea didn't work because the *Mona Lisa* was painted on wood. Maybe you can write a new solution to the problem: How would the characters steal it?

Trina Schart Hyman

Born: April 8, 1939, in Philadelphia, Pennsylvania
Home: Lyme, New Hampshire

SELECTED TITLES

Self-Portrait: Trina Schart Hyman
1981

Rapunzel
1982

Little Red Riding Hood
(Caldecott Honor Book)
1983

Saint George and the Dragon
(Caldecott Medal)
1984

A Child's Christmas in Wales
1985

Hershel and the Hanukkah Goblins
(Caldecott Honor Book)
1989

The Fortune-Tellers
1992

Winter Poems
1994

A Child's Calendar
(Caldecott Honor Book)
1999

The Serpent Slayer and Other Stories of Strong Women
2000

Trina Schart Hyman has always preferred the world of the imagination to the "real world" of shopping malls, newspapers, and television sets.

Growing up in a rural area 20 miles north of Philadelphia, Trina and her younger sister, Karleen, would play games about fairies and imaginary kingdoms. To Trina, "They were more real to us than anything we could really see."

Trina's favorite books were fairy tale, folktale, and mythology collections—anything that could transport her, through her imagination, to a new world. She explains, "It's a chance to take your head and go to another place—another world, another time, another way of feeling."

Perhaps Trina inherited her love of fantasy from her father, a man who loved music, singing, and long walks. "My father told the best stories," Trina wrote in her autobiography, *Self-Portrait: Trina Schart Hyman*. "He sometimes took me for walks at night and told me long magical stories of the origins of the stars. My father's made-up mythology is still much more interesting than the stories the scientists have invented."

A Born Illustrator

Call it an active imagination, a sense of wonder, or simply the ability to dream. Whatever you choose to name it, Trina Schart Hyman was born with a unique talent. She is able to see characters and places in her imagination—and share those visions with others through her art. Illustrating books was the perfect career. Trina confesses, "I don't think I could do anything else. I had to be an artist."

Trina doesn't believe that a person can decide to become an artist. "Real artists don't say, How do I get to be an artist? That's like saying Gee, how do I get to have brown eyes? I really think you

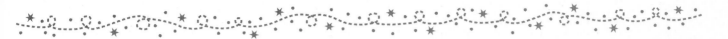

either are or you aren't." She does, however, offer this advice: "I tell kids to keep on drawing, keep on painting, keep on making pictures. It doesn't matter how you do it; it matters a lot *how often* you do it."

Though Trina has written some books, she mainly works as an illustrator. Once she agrees to illustrate a manuscript—it has to, as she puts it, "ring my chimes"—the work begins.

- -

"I like kids better than I like grown-ups. They are just a lot easier to talk to and be with. And they are a lot more fun."

- -

Trina helps the creative process along by taking long walks each morning. She calls it her thinking time. During these walks, the pictures begin to take shape in her mind. "I don't normally do a lot of sketches, because the illustrations and the whole flow of the book are very clear in my head before I start."

But it's never easy to get the pictures out of her mind and onto the paper. Trina admits, "There are some days when I go to sit down at my drawing table and I just want to cry. Sometimes I do cry. But I've learned to keep working—even if I'm messing up

and making mistakes."

Trina usually works from ten o'clock in the morning to eight o'clock at night. "If I didn't discipline myself, I just wouldn't work. I'd much rather hang out and fool around. So many people say to me, 'Oh what a fun job, it must be so much fun!' They think I just sort of sit down and goof around. But it's hard work!"

Of her own books, Trina's favorites are *How Does It Feel to Be Old?* and *Little Red Riding Hood*. *Little Red Riding Hood* holds a particularly special place in her heart. The story was a childhood favorite, one her mother used to read aloud to her over and over again.

Trina remembers, "It was so much a part of me that I actually became Little Red Riding Hood. My mother sewed me a red satin cape with a hood that I wore almost every day. My dog, Tippy, was the wolf."

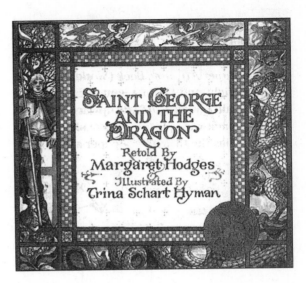

DO IT YOURSELF!

Self-Portrait: Trina Schart Hyman provides readers with interesting information about the artist. Perhaps you'd like to write your own autobiography. Try organizing the information into sections; for example: Home, Family, School, Friends. You decide what to write—it's your life! Just be sure to include illustrations or photographs.

Tony Johnston

Born: January 30, 1942, in Los Angeles, California
Home: San Marino, California

SELECTED TITLES

The Vanishing Pumpkin
1983

The Quilt Story
1985

Whale Song
1987

Yonder
1988

The Badger and the Magic Fan: A Japanese Folktale
1990

Grandpa's Song
1991

The Cowboy and the Black-Eyed Pea
1992

The Tale of Rabbit and Coyote
1994

The Iguana Brothers
1995

Bigfoot Cinderrrrrella
1998

It's About Dogs
2000

Tony Johnston is excited about a story. You can hear it in her voice. This is the part of the job she really loves—the thrill of a new idea and the challenge of making it all fall into place.

As she describes her story, Tony tells us a lot about the way she works. "I was in Tulsa," Tony says, "and heard an interesting fact about the Muscogee [Creek] tribe. When they were forced from their land in Alabama on a march to Tulsa in the 1830s, they brought living embers with them. The tribe relit the embers each night to remind them of their homeland."

Tony, who is part Cherokee and has a deep interest in Native American life, knew there was a story there somewhere. Bursting with thoughts, she quickly jotted down a rough first draft. "That's the way I work," Tony says. "I try to grab the feeling when the idea strikes. I think I wrote most of the ember story on the airplane barf bag going home!" Tony believes that in writing any story, the writer's own feelings must be fully engaged. She explains, "If you get in touch with your emotions, you can write a first draft really without doing any research, then go back and fill it in. For me, going to the library and facing a mountain of research would get in the way of the creative process."

> **"I think of myself as a soup pot. You throw all of this stuff into the pot and let it blub around, and just maybe you'll end up with a good soup!"**

With a first draft in her hands, Tony can move on to the next stage. In this case it meant doing some homework. Tony had a lot of questions she needed answered. She offers an example: "I wanted to know what a person from that tribe would have thought while standing at a grave site. If he were burying a relative, what would he be thinking? Who would he pray

68

to? I know what a white person might think, but I don't know about a Creek." For help, Tony contacted the Muscogee tribe. The elders agreed to answer her questions. Tony got the information she needed for the story.

But that's only one story of many that are constantly in the works. When asked what else she's been up to lately, Tony answers with a laugh, "Oh, about 85 different things. I've always got a lot going. I mean, I've got a whole lot of good beginnings without middles or endings."

From Teacher to Writer

A former teacher, Tony used to create stories with her fourth-grade class. One day a friend encouraged Tony to try to get her stories published. "At the time, it hadn't occurred to me to become a children's book writer," she says. "I thought, Well, how do you do it? I tried to figure out what makes one book wonderful and another only fair. And, of course, I'm still trying to figure that out."

A lot of Tony's writing time is actually spent rewriting. "I revise and revise and revise," she says. "I'm so picky. *Yonder* took me seven years to write. That book meant a lot to me. I wanted it to be perfect." Tony does not illustrate her books, so she depends on her editor to select an artist who will do a good job at bringing her words to life. Tony has been fortunate to work with such great illustrators as Tomie dePaola, Lillian Hoban, Ed Young, Margot Tomes, Leo Politi, Victoria Chess, and Mark Teague. To each one, she is grateful.

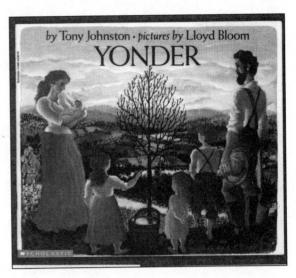

by Tony Johnston · pictures by Lloyd Bloom
YONDER

It becomes clear in speaking with Tony that *Yonder* holds special meaning for her. She tries to explain why. "I cried for about seven years while I was writing that book. Everything that you write is autobiographical. I don't care if it's about snakes or iguanas, it is always rooted in something that means something to you. *Yonder* evokes so many things from my childhood. I spent a lot of time on a ranch growing up. I was very close to my grandparents. Somehow I tried to put all of that family feeling into the book. One of my grandparents, Addie, was from Texas. Whenever I would ask, 'Grandma, where's my sister?' she would answer, 'Yonder.' When I started writing, that word triggered more and more memories."

DO IT YOURSELF!

Tony Johnston talks about her "drawer of dreams," the secret place where she keeps all her thoughts, dreams, and manuscripts. Find your own special place—it can be a box, drawer, folder, journal—where you can keep your ideas and cherished objects. Who knows, you may open it one day and find a story waiting for you!

Ezra Jack Keats

Born: March 11, 1916, in Brooklyn, New York
Died: May 6, 1983

SELECTED TITLES

The Snowy Day
(Caldecott Medal)
1962

Whistle for Willie
1964

John Henry,
an American Legend
1965

A Letter to Amy
1968

The Little Drummer Boy
1968

Goggles!
(Caldecott Honor Book)
1969

Hi, Cat!
1970

Apt. 3
1971

Over in the Meadow
1971

Regards to the Man
in the Moon
1981

When asked where he got his ideas for books, Ezra Jack Keats said with a wink, "Well, as an editor of mine once said, I'm an ex-kid."

In a way, Keats never did grow up. Even in his sixties, he remembered his childhood as if it were yesterday. He remembered the sights, the sounds, the smells of the city. And his books celebrated the richness, the beauty, and the mystery of a child's life in the city.

Ezra Jack Keats's parents traveled to America from Poland and settled in a poor section of Brooklyn. As a child he showed an early interest in painting. His mother took great pride in his work. She even let him get away with things that most mothers would not. "I drew on and colored in everything that came across my path," Ezra said.

Once he drew all over his kitchen table. "I filled up the entire table with pictures of little cottages, curly smoke coming out of the chimneys, men's profiles, and kids."

Ezra Jack was happily doodling away when his mother suddenly entered the room. "I expected her to say, 'What have you been doing?' and 'Get that sponge and wipe it off!' Instead she looked at me and said, 'Did you do that? Isn't it wonderful!'"

"The gray background for the pages where Peter goes to sleep (in The Snowy Day) was made by splattering India ink with a toothbrush."

His father, however, tried to discourage Ezra Jack from becoming a painter. When Ezra Jack was painting, his father would say, "Get out and play ball and stop making a fool of yourself!" One day he pulled Ezra Jack aside and said, "Never be an artist—you'll have a terrible life."

But Keats didn't listen. He kept painting away. Slowly, over time, his father realized that Ezra Jack had a special talent. He was so impressed, he took Ezra Jack to the Metropolitan Museum of Art. It would be a day that Ezra Jack would never forget, for it opened his eyes to the magical possibilities of art. But most important, he learned that his father was proud of his painting.

Keats began his career by illustrating children's books written by other authors. He liked the books he was asked to illustrate, but Ezra was worried. Something, he thought, was missing.

A Black Hero

"I never got a story about black people, black children. I decided that if I did a book of my own, my hero would be a black child." That book was *The Snowy Day*. It was, according to *Horn Book* magazine, "the very first full-color picture book to feature a small black hero."

It was a simple story about his own childhood experience. Keats said: "It tells about the excitement I felt as a boy when I woke up to see snow outside the Brooklyn apartment where I grew up."

It really didn't matter whether the star of *The Snowy Day*, Peter, was black or white. The book captured something magical for all children—the wonder and joy of a silent winter snowfall. Keats remarked, "I had been illustrating

books by other people showing the goodness of white children, and in my own book I wanted to show and share the beauty and goodness of the black child."

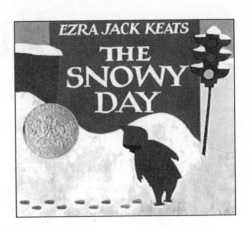

The Snowy Day won the Caldecott Medal for the best illustrated book of the year. In addition to paint, Keats used scraps of wool, colored paper, scissors, and glue to create beautiful collages.

To make his books, Keats spent days sketching and photographing city streets and children. Then he used these pictures to create his illustrations. When he completed the illustrations, he would hang them on his wall. If the characters seemed to be talking to him, he knew the illustrations were right. Ezra Jack Keats believed that good pictures wrote their own stories.

In 1983 Ezra Jack Keats died of a heart attack. But he left his readers with a gift. Books, he told us, should be for all people. He said, "Let us open the book covers to new and wonderful, true and inspiring stories for all children, about all children—the tall and short, fat and thin, dark and light, beautiful and homely. Welcome!"

DO IT YOURSELF!

Study the work of Ezra Jack Keats, and then make your own collage using scissors, paper, glue, and paints. Just remember this tip from the artist: "The edges of shapes are varied in several ways. Sharp edges are made by cutting, rough edges by tearing, soft edges by painting over them."

Steven Kellogg

Born: October 26, 1941, in Norwalk, Connecticut
Home: Sandy Hook, Connecticut

SELECTED TITLES

Can I Keep Him?
1971

The Boy Who Was Followed Home
1975

The Mysterious Tadpole
1977

Pinkerton, Behave!
1979

The Day Jimmy's Boa Ate the Wash
1980

Paul Bunyan: A Tall Tale
1984

How Much Is a Million?
1985

Pecos Bill
1986

I Was Born About 10,000 Years Ago
1996

A Beasty Story
1999

Give the Dog a Bone
2000

There are few things that author-illustrator Steven Kellogg enjoys more than taking a leisurely romp through the woods. Says Kellogg, "The woods are very relaxing and very peaceful. Taking walks encourages me to step inside myself in a calm, thoughtful way. Just rambling through the woodland paths, thinking about stories and images—it's a good way to make progress on my work away from the drawing board."

Surprisingly, Kellogg rarely takes a sketchbook along with him. For Steven, it's purely a time to think, feel, and observe nature. "I'm always doing visual homework," he explains. "I know some artists use models when they draw, but I don't. But I'm always storing up images and expressions in my memory file that I can flip through and draw upon when I'm actually working on a book.

"Part of what artists do is inspire everyone to be more observant, to be more aware of the world around us. Once we take things for granted, we stop seeing—we stop appreciating the wonder of the visual world."

When it comes time to work, Kellogg secludes himself in his favorite place—a specially designed studio. "I have a really terrific room in my house that I have had for about 10 years, though I had dreamed of having it built for about 25 years. It's at the very top of the house and it has all sorts of wonderful roof angles and skylights overlooking the treetops. I love it. It's like a world of its own."

Telling Stories on Paper

As a child Steven loved books and stories about dinosaurs and dragons. He not only enjoyed reading stories but also liked making them up. "I had this process, called telling stories on paper, where I would make up stories for my two younger sisters. I scribbled pictures as I talked, sitting between my sisters with a big stack of paper on my

lap," Kellogg recalls. Then, laughing, he adds: "It's essentially what I'm doing now."

"Making a book is like making a friend. You give different sides of yourself to each book, and each book gives different things back to you. Each one is a very special experience."

Perhaps because Steven is both a writer and an illustrator, he believes that words and pictures are equally important. "I think of it as a duet," he says. "Words and pictures are like two voices, singing different melodies. Together, they blend to make it more beautiful and more meaningful than either voice could be on its own."

But sometimes, Kellogg admits, it can take years to create a book's "beautiful music." That's because Kellogg is a perfectionist. He refuses to let a book go to the publisher before he's completely satisfied. He confesses, "I'm very aware of the fact that once the book is printed, there's no hope for revision. One of my real terrors is to look back at something and think, You should have stuck with that longer; it's not as good as it could have been."

It comes as no surprise, then, to learn that Steven Kellogg revises his work up until the very last moment. No matter how much time he's put into a project, he always finds things that can be improved. "I'm constantly rethinking, refining, reworking, rearranging. That's the process by which the book finds its right momentum from beginning to end."

Young readers often write to Steven Kellogg asking if he likes his job. Steven says, "I relate to that question very much. As a child I was very aware that many adults hated their jobs. I was determined even then to choose a job that I'd enjoy. When I visit schools, I tell kids that it's important to get to know yourself as well as you can, because then you can choose the job and lifestyle that's right for you."

CAN I KEEP HIM?
STORY AND PICTURES BY
STEVEN KELLOGG

DO IT YOURSELF!

Steven Kellogg's book *Can I Keep Him?* is about a boy's wish to adopt a pet, any kind of pet: a bear, a lion, even a dinosaur! Try writing a story about what would happen if you were allowed to keep a dinosaur for a pet.

Karla Kuskin

Born: July 17, 1932, in New York, New York
Home: Brooklyn, New York

Can you imagine what it feels like to be the last leaf on a tree in autumn, silently letting go and drifting to the ground? Can you imagine what it feels like to be a snake, a strawberry, or a sled? Karla Kuskin can.

Karla often plays pretend to help her write poems. In an introduction to one of her books, *Any Me I Want to Be*, Karla explains the process this way: "Instead of describing how a cat, the moon, or a pair of shoes appears to me, I have tried to get inside each subject and briefly be it."

Karla feels that this imaginary activity is a great way to learn. She says, "If you are able to imagine being someone else, it helps you see the world through someone else's eyes." Our imagination, Karla emphasizes, allows us to realize that different lives are just as valuable as our own.

Through sense and silliness, bouncy rhymes and flowing rhythms, Karla shares her love of poetry with young children. A mood, a memory, a sound— anything can spark a poem. And anyone can write one, Karla believes. "Poetry can be as natural and effective a form of

self-expression as singing or shouting," she says.

Karla has always loved listening to the rhythm of words. She states, "I am a firm believer in reading aloud because, I suppose, I loved it so much as a child." Grateful for a childhood in which reading was an everyday family activity, Karla believes that "when you are exposed to poetry when you are little, it stays with you for the rest of your life.

"When I am working on a book of poetry," Karla says, "I jot down everything on any scrap of paper at hand; I pay attention to what's going through my head. I'm much more aware of language, words, rhythm, description. I try to hang on to these ideas, because if I don't write them down, they're gone forever."

It is Karla's hope that readers of her poems will, in turn, write poems of their own. As she says,

"If you read, you write." Karla realizes, though, that most children will not grow up to become professional writers. "The important thing about writing," she says, "is that it helps the writer discover his or her own thoughts and feelings.

> **"If you really keep your eyes open and you really listen to language, you discover that there's a tremendous amount of beauty in the world."**

"In difficult times," Karla confides, "I've always found that to write out what I feel is very helpful. I put it down and I begin to understand it better."

Working With Words

In its basic form, revision is a simple process of messing around with words. The writer takes words away, eliminates unnecessary paragraphs, smoothes out rhythms, searches for the very best word. Yet revision is more than just tinkering around with language. It is sometimes a matter of looking at an old story or poem with new eyes. It can be a time to make sweeping changes—rethink the plot, change the setting, introduce new characters. This process helped Karla Kuskin finally publish one of her most popular

books, *The Philharmonic Gets Dressed*.

Karla remembers: "When I first wrote *The Philharmonic Gets Dressed*, I wrote it with only one musician and it wasn't interesting. I put the manuscript away for a couple of years. Then all of a sudden I realized the book might work if it was about the whole orchestra."

Once married to an oboe player, Karla got the idea by noticing her children watch their father get dressed for work. She wanted to present these gifted musicians as regular people with real jobs—just like carpenters, bus drivers, and football players.

"What I was saying was: Here are people who get up, get washed, get dressed—just like you do—but what they do for work is heavenly. But it isn't play. It is real, true, serious work."

Maybe the same can be said for children's authors like Karla Kuskin. They awake in the morning, eat breakfast, wash the dishes, and go off to work. Their work is to imagine and feel, to write and draw, to create beautiful books. Not a bad job if you can get it. But, as Karla might point out, it's still work.

by Karla Kuskin
illustrations by Marc Simont

DO IT YOURSELF!

Karla wrote notes to accompany her poems in *Near the Window Tree*. These notes show where she got some of the ideas for her poems. Try taking some notes yourself—maybe it will help start a poem or two! Karla sometimes looks to a tree for inspiration: "Once in a while I look out at the tree in the yard. Then I look at the blank paper on my lap and I try to get the tree to give me an idea for something to write about."

Leo Lionni

Born: May 5, 1910, in Amsterdam, Holland
Died: October 11, 1999

SELECTED TITLES

Inch by Inch
(Caldecott Honor Book)
1960

Swimmy
(Caldecott Honor Book)
1963

Frederick
(Caldecott Honor Book)
1967

Alexander and the Wind-Up Mouse
(Caldecott Honor Book)
1969

Fish Is Fish
1970

Theodore and the Talking Mushroom
1971

A Color of His Own
1975

Cornelius
1983

It's Mine!
1986

Matthew's Dream
1991

A Busy Year
1992

Leo Lionni passed away in the fall of 1999, leaving behind an enduring and beloved collection of work. His books have earned a long list of awards, including the Lewis Carroll Shelf Award and four Caldecott Honors. Lionni's books remain singular, personal, one-of-a-kind. He was a rare and insightful writer, employing language that was at once clear, spare, and elegant.

On the surface his books are simple and childlike: tales of bickering crocodiles, dreamy mice, and clever caterpillars. His artwork is masterful, featuring stylized collages, watery washes, and flat-shaped animals. Yet within Lionni's books there is extraordinary depth. Below the surface story, which is often a simple fable, layers of meaning lay submerged. In this way Lionni provided teachers and children with perfect "talking books," for reading them is never enough. The books, in the hands of the curious, often elicit sparkling conversations and lively debate. In short, Lionni wrote books that make readers—of any age—*think.*

Lionni was born in Amsterdam, Holland. He determined early on to become an artist. "I lived within two blocks of two of the best museums of Europe," Lionni recalled. "I spent most of my time there and quite naturally assumed that one day I would become an artist. In grade school nature studies were very important to me. I remember how we collected plants and kept all sorts of animals. I relive these early experiences over and over again." Thinking back on his childhood, Lionni concluded, "I haven't changed very much."

In 1939, at the onset of World War II, Lionni fled from Europe to the United States and found work as an art director for a large advertising agency. An accomplished sculptor, writer, and photographer, Lionni turned his attention to painting in the mid-1940s, eventually exhibiting his work in one-man shows throughout the States and Europe.

His entrance into the world of children's books, by Lionni's own admission, "just happened." While traveling by train with his grandchildren, Lionni conjured a story about two torn circles to keep them entertained. He later turned this material into his first book, *Little Blue and Little Yellow*.

> ### "My stories are meant to stimulate the mind, to create an awareness, to destroy a prejudice."

Lionni's books are not so much for children as they are for the child in all of us. He mused, "I believe that a good children's book should appeal to all people who have not completely lost their original joy and wonder in life. The fact is that I really don't make books for children at all. I make them for that part of us, of myself and of my friends, that has never changed, that is still child."

Fresh and uncluttered, Lionni's simple fables explore deeper themes such as individuality and self-reliance, and a longing for community. They gave the artist a profound sense of accomplishment. He reflected, "Among the varied things I have done in my life, few have given me more and greater satisfaction than my children's books."

Lionni once explained, "The protagonist of my books is often an individual who is, because of special circumstances, an outcast, a rebel, a victim, or a hero. His story ends happily because of his intelligence, his vitality and resourcefulness, his goodness, or simply because his will and patience turn the laws of averages to his advantage. Often he has to learn through suffering, but it is always his own vitality, his discovery that life is a positive, exciting fact, that makes him come out on top."

Leo Lionni's most deeply personal book is *Frederick*, a fable that stresses the importance of the artist to society. In the book, a group of field mice gather food for the harsh winter ahead—all except for Frederick, who dreams the days away, soaking in the sunshine, the smells of summer, the colors of the world. Come the dark, dreary days of winter, Frederick makes his own valuable—and surprising—contribution to the struggling mouse community. The gift that Frederick offers, like Lionni himself, is not food or shelter. It is the gift of art—something that feeds our inner world and sustains us all.

DO IT YOURSELF!

Leo Lionni readily admitted, "My characters are humans in disguise, and their little problems and situations are human problems, human situations." Try it yourself. Think of an incident in your own life and write about it. But when writing, use animals as the characters. Instead of an argument between you and your sister, for example, turn the characters into two mewling cats or two frogs on a lily pad. See how this changes the story. And also notice how some elements stay the same.

Arnold Lobel

Born: May 22, 1933, in Los Angeles, California
Died: December 4, 1987

SELECTED TITLES

Frog and Toad Are Friends
(Caldecott Honor Book)
1970

Hildilid's Night
(Caldecott Honor Book)
1971

Frog and Toad Together
(Newbery Honor Book)
1972

Mouse Tales
1972

Grasshopper on the Road
1978

Fables
(Caldecott Medal)
1980

*Ming Lo Moves
the Mountain*
1982

*The Book of Pigericks:
Pig Limericks*
1983

Whiskers and Rhymes
1985

*The Random House
Book of Mother Goose*
1986

The first time Arnold Lobel tried to draw a grasshopper, he failed miserably. He looked at what he drew and thought, That doesn't look like a grasshopper at all; that looks like a green rabbit! But he kept at it, drawing and redrawing his grasshopper. Finally, after much hard work, he succeeded. Today you can read about Lobel's grasshopper in the book *Grasshopper on the Road*.

Yes, even the legendary Arnold Lobel failed at times. But his willingness to fail and then try again may have been the secret to his success.

Arnold Lobel was born in Los Angeles and grew up in Schenectady, New York. He recalled: "From my house the long walk to the library was downhill all the way. I would return the books I had borrowed and would quickly stock up on five new selections. Five, as I remember, was the most books that one could take out at a time."

Arnold studied fine arts in college and discovered that he had a talent for illustrating books. In 1959 he got his first break. An editor at a publishing house liked a drawing of a cricket that Arnold

had made. "Can you draw a salmon?" she asked. Arnold, who had never tried to draw a salmon, fibbed and said, "Oh yes, I do it all the time!" That day he got a job: illustrating the children's book *Red Tag Comes Home*.

Drawing Upon His Life

Lobel believed that a writer or illustrator must draw upon the events in his or her own life. Books, he said, "have to come out of the things that I, as an author, am passionately interested in." What did interest Arnold Lobel? His cat, Orson, for one. Lobel loved his cat. While Arnold worked at his drawing table, Orson would hop right up to rub noses with him. Then Orson would stretch, yawn, and sit down right on top of the illustration Arnold was working on. Maybe that's why cats appear so frequently in his books!

The most famous example of Arnold using his own life as a source of ideas is with the Frog and Toad books. While vacationing in Vermont, Lobel's two children returned home with a bucketful of frogs and toads they had caught. Gradually an idea formed for a book about two best friends, a frog and a toad.

"One of the secrets of writing good books for children is that you can't really write books for children; you must write books for yourself and about yourself."

Lobel delighted in putting elements of his own life in his books. Read the opening limerick in *The Book of Pigericks* to find out how far he'd go to "put himself" into each story:

There was an old pig with a pen
Who wrote stories and verse now
  and then.
To enhance these creations,
He drew illustrations
With brushes, some paints
and his pen.

If you look at the illustration on page 8 of that book, you'll see a pig hard at work at a drawing table. Somehow the pig, wearing glasses and a mustache, seems oddly familiar. Now take a look at a picture of Lobel. Notice any similarities? The pig is Arnold Lobel's creative idea of a self-portrait!

Writing, for Arnold Lobel, was much more difficult than drawing pictures. He said, "Sitting in a chair with an open notebook on my lap, waiting for nothing to happen, is not my idea of fun.

"The creation of most picture books for children is not dramatic," Lobel said in his acceptance speech for the prestigious Caldecott Medal. "It is a matter of daily, patient, single-minded effort. It is a matter of writing words on a page in a silent room."

Sadly, Arnold Lobel suffered a long illness before he died in December 1987. Yet as he battled his disease each day, he created new books—until the very end of his life.

Once, while looking at what he knew would be his last book, *The Turnaround Wind*, Arnold Lobel happily said: "I can't believe I did what I did." Many of his readers have the same reaction: It's hard to believe that one man could contribute so much.

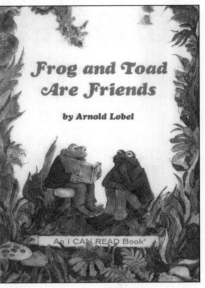

DO IT YOURSELF!

In *The Book of Pigericks*, Arnold Lobel took a traditional form of writing (the limerick) and gave it a twist. See if you can write your own pigericks. Or perhaps you'd like to try moosericks or dogericks? Begin by finding out the rules, or proper form, for limericks. If you fail the first time, don't give up. Arnold Lobel never did!

Jonathan London

Born: March 11, 1947, in Brooklyn, New York
Home: Graton, California

SELECTED TITLES

Froggy Gets Dressed
(first in a series)
1992

The Lion Who Had Asthma
1992

Thirteen Moons on Turtle's Back
1992

The Eyes of Gray Wolf
1993

Fire Race: A Karuk Coyote Tale
1993

Hip Cat
1993

Like Butter on Pancakes
1995

What Newt Could Do for Turtle
1996

Wiggle Waggle
(first in a series)
1999

Who Bop?
2000

What Do You Love?
2000

Jonathan London loves frogs and mud and the silent wonder of animals in the wild. He loves thunderstorms and puddles and the shivery dark of night. He loves words that take strange shape in his mouth, like *squelch*, and words that make kids giggle, like *zap* and *flop* and, yes, even *underwear*.

But more than anything, Jonathan loves writing about what he loves. His books are, at their very core, celebrations. Jonathan explains, "The feeling I get when I am at my best is exuberance, elation, joy. I do think that my books celebrate life, in whatever version it comes out."

The impulse to write comes from Jonathan's basic need to share his experiences, thoughts, and dreams. He muses, "I don't know why, but I don't feel like I'm experiencing something fully if I'm not sharing it. If I am off alone—hiking, or whatever—the first thing I think of is, Oh, I wish my wife, Maureen, or my children, Aaron and Sean, were here to see this. Then I go back home and share it. It's how I am. So I think the writing is an extension of that."

Like breathing air, writing is simply something that Jonathan

London *does*. For many years he wrote countless poems and stories—always for adults. "I never thought about writing for kids," London admits. "What changed for me was having kids of my own. When they were little, they asked me to tell them stories. I didn't realize that I was a storyteller, but stories would pop out and I would tell them."

Jonathan's first book came directly from that personal, intimate father-and-child experience. "My first book that I actually wrote down and sold was a lullaby story that I told to my son, Sean, when he was two," London says. The story, *The Owl Who Became the Moon*, was accepted for publication. Suddenly, almost by accident, Jonathon London was a children's book author. He never looked back.

"I felt like I was walking 13 inches above the ground,"

Jonathan gleefully recounts. "From then on, I turned all my writing attention to kids."

> **"I spent several years traveling around the world, meeting people of different cultures and writing poems. Gradually the goal of becoming a writer took root and didn't let go."**

Jonathan London is best known for his popular Froggy stories. The first was *Froggy Gets Dressed*. After reading it to a group of children and watching them literally roll on the floor with laughter, Jonathan knew he had written something special.

Jonathan recalls, "That story literally popped out of my head while driving back from a hiking trip with my kids. They said, 'Tell me a story.' The story wrote itself as I told it. I'm pretty sure that my youngest son, Sean, came up with the underwear idea. I didn't know what was going to come next. I didn't plan it out. I went home and wrote it in about an hour."

Ideas, like far-flung visitors, come to Jonathan from a variety of places. Some come from personal experience; others emerge from dreams. *Thirteen Moons on Turtle's Back*, coauthored by Joseph Bruchac, grew directly from a

dream. London explains, "I only remembered that there were moons and that they had names: 'the moon of joyful roundness,' and 'the moon of hazy sorrow.' The dream-moons made me think of Native American moons. I knew instantly that I wanted to do a book about the moons."

But Jonathan insists, "I don't like to be limited by experience or dreams. I catch words and ideas that seem to fly through the air. *Hip cat*, those two words, became a story because I heard those words as a child might. Soon I had a story in mind about a cat who plays the saxophone and wants to become a jazz musician."

London concludes, "There are worlds of possibilities living within your imagination, from which you can create stories that can make someone want to cry or laugh, play a saxophone, or make a snowman. This act of writing, for me, is a part of my celebration of life, a way to give back a little for all that I have been given."

DO IT YOURSELF!

Jonathan London has often used dream memories as a source of inspiration. In the morning, before rushing out of bed, linger for a moment and try to remember your dreams. Think about them. Maybe there's an idea floating around in your imagination, waiting for you to recognize it.

James Marshall

Born: October 10, 1942, in San Antonio, Texas
Died: October 13, 1992

SELECTED TITLES

George and Martha
(first in a series)
1972

The Stupids Step Out
(first in a series)
1974

*Mary Alice,
Operator Number 9*
1975

Miss Nelson Is Missing!
(first in a series)
1977

Portly McSwine
1979

Three by the Sea
1981

Red Riding Hood
1987

*Goldilocks and the
Three Bears*
(Caldecott Honor Book)
1988

Hansel and Gretel
1990

Ideas for James Marshall's books usually began with daydreams and doodles. While sketching, Marshall would often discover some very interesting—and quite unexpected—characters. He explained, "The story develops out of the character's personality. For me, as an illustrator, it often comes from what will look funny. The idea of a character pouring soup into his loafers is a funny kind of thing. It's visually funny. The words come to me later."

Still, James Marshall was reluctant to claim that he completely understood his own creative process. "An author or illustrator can point out the mysteries, or the magic, or even the silliness of the world. But to me it doesn't come out of the author; the author explores something that already exists. I didn't make up the things that are funny in my books. I just see them, recognize them, and pass them along. It doesn't really matter where the ideas come from."

Like the work of all great illustrators, there is no mistaking Marshall's work for anyone else's. You look at a plump hippopotamus lazily lounging in a tub and you know it can only be the work of Marshall.

Part of the reason James Marshall had a unique style is that he was a self-taught artist. "I'm glad that I never went to art school," he said, "because had I gone I probably would have ended up copying the style of other illustrators. People love a Maurice Sendak or an Arnold Lobel book because of the special, very individual vision they bring to their work. This is why the artists I love are not the cool technicians but those who have a vision to share with others."

Almost Normal

James Marshall was born and raised in Texas. He lived on a sprawling, 85-acre farm outside of San Antonio. He was an only child until he was 12 years old. As a result, Marshall reflected, "like many children who are

alone a great deal, I had to fall back on my own resources. I lived in my imagination."

- -

"If I don't have a good character, then I don't have a book."

- -

Marshall's childhood was "almost" normal. He did, however, have one peculiar habit. Laughing, Marshall recalled, "My sister reminded me that as a kid I used to hide toast. I hated toast. So instead of eating it, I would hide it. The closet in my bedroom was stacked with toast!"

Later in his career, Marshall divided his time between two homes—one in Mansield Hollow, Connecticut, and one in Manhattan. He did most of his work in his Connecticut studio. But there was always a sketchbook nearby in case he got in a creative mood.

"The real trick," Marshall confided in an interview, "is to find your own personal working rhythms— your own way of working."

While many illustrators keep conventional hours, working from nine to five, Marshall preferred to work at night— sometimes late into the wee hours. "The later, the better," he claimed. "My ideas are usually fresher and funnier at night."

What did James Marshall consider

the hardest part of creating a picture book? "It's always the ending that gives me the most trouble," Marshall admitted. "The ending," he said, "is what people remember. If the book fizzles at the end, they remember the whole thing as a fizzled book. It's important to have a very satisfying ending for the reader. They've entered a world and now they are leaving it. So it's a puzzle that has to be solved. I remember with one of the Miss Nelson books, it took us [the author Harry Allard and I] two years to come up with an ending we liked!"

written and illustrated by
JAMES MARSHALL

James Marshall died in 1992, but he remains an influential voice in children's literature. Even today he is often named as a favorite of a new generation of authors and illustrators, ranging from Tedd Arnold to Dav Pilkey. Through his beloved children's books and memorable characters, James provided readers with the gift of laughter.

DO IT YOURSELF!

James Marshall believed that reading enriches the imagination. Asked to suggest an activity that will help kids enjoy his books, Marshall said, "I'd like to see kids read my books, then sit back and just daydream. After all, daydreaming is important—I've practically made a career out of it." Sounds like good advice indeed. Ready, set, daydream!

Bill Martin, Jr.

Born: March 20, 1916, in Hiawatha, Kansas
Home: New York, New York

SELECTED TITLES

Brown Bear, Brown Bear, What Do You See?
1971

The Ghost-Eye Tree
1985

Barn Dance!
1986

White Dynamite and Curly Kidd
1986

Here Are My Hands
1987

Knots on a Counting Rope
1987

Chicka Chicka Boom Boom
1989

The Magic Pumpkin
1989

The Happy Hippopotami
1991

Old Devil Wind
1993

A Beasty Story
1999

Born in 1916, Bill Martin, Jr. remembers growing up in the days before television, when kids had to create their own entertainment. Bill vividly recalls, "On long summer nights the kids in the neighborhood would sit on the curb underneath the street lights, telling stories to one another. Most of them were ghost stories. We loved those."

Bill wrote his first book as a favor to his brother, Bernard, who was an artist. "I was in the army," Bill recalls. "It was 1944. My brother had been injured in the service. He wrote to me and said, 'Why don't you write me a children's story so I can illustrate it while I'm recuperating?' I said, 'Sure.'" One Sunday Bill sat down at the typewriter and banged out a story called *The Little Squeegy Bug.* Bernard liked it, illustrated it, and had it published!

Encouraged by this success, Bill and Bernard started their own publishing company. But Bill soon realized that he didn't know enough about children. So he went off to school to study early childhood education. After graduation Bill became a principal at an elementary school. In 1960 he joined the publishing house of

Holt, Rinehart & Winston as an editor and creator of educational reading materials.

"I started writing the kinds of things that I thought children needed," Bill says. "I wanted children to become page-turners. I wanted them to be able to read a book in five minutes, so they could proudly say, 'I read a book.' Children love to have power over books. When a frail reader finds a book that he or she can read, it's such a triumph that the reader will read it again and again and again."

Brown Bear and More

More often than not, good writing is a result of hard work and endless revision. But sometimes, amazingly, the words flow easily and they are exactly right from the very beginning. Bill recalls one such instance: "I was on the

train one day, coming into work from suburban New York. I heard, 'Brown bear, brown bear, what do you see?' So I wrote it down. Having no tablet with me, I wrote it on the newspaper. Then I wrote, 'I see a red bird looking at me.' Then I wrote down 'yellow duck,' 'blue horse,' 'green frog,' 'purple cat,' 'white dog,' et cetera. Within 15 minutes the story was complete."

"No reading lesson is complete unless it leaves children with the sharp taste of words lingering on their tongues."

Excited, Bill typed up the story when he reached the office. Now he needed to find an illustrator. Thumbing through a magazine, Bill was struck by an ad for a pharmaceutical company. "It had a collage of a beautiful pink lobster," Bill recalls. "I said to myself, 'That's the guy who should illustrate the book.'"

The name of the illustrator was Eric Carle. At the time he had never done a children's book. Bill asked Eric: "Are you interested in illustrating a children's book?" Eric cautiously answered: "Probably so." And that is the story of how the great Eric Carle, author of *The Very Hungry Caterpillar*, got his start in children's books.

One of Bill's most popular books, *Chicka Chicka Boom Boom*, cowritten with frequent collaborator John Archambault, features a jazzy rhyme that invites children to read along and share the experience. Many writers talk about how it often takes years for an idea to become a fully developed book. That was the case with *Chicka Chicka Boom Boom*. Bill explains, "*Chicka Chicka Boom Boom* was carried around as a single line in our journals for a couple of years. We didn't do anything with it; it just sort of slept there."

Weeks, months, and years passed. One day Bill got a call from a publisher who needed a story for a textbook—and fast. Though Bill didn't have any stories ready to offer, he promised to deliver one in two weeks. He recalls, "I opened my journal and rediscovered that line: *A told B and B told C, I'll race you to the top of the coconut tree.*" Needless to say, Bill and John delivered the book on time.

by Bill Martin, Jr. and John Archambault

illustrated by Lois Ehlert

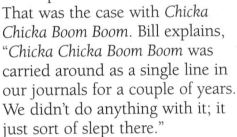

DO IT YOURSELF!

Like Bill Martin, Jr. and John Archambault, try writing with a partner. You'll need to share ideas until you agree on what the story should be about. One approach might be to write it as a dialogue, like *Knots on a Counting Rope*. Each writer can take on the voice of a character. As you write, continue to share ideas and make suggestions to improve the story. Remember, respect and cooperation are essential parts of the process.

Jean Marzollo

Born: June 24, 1942, in Manchester, Connecticut
Home: Cold Spring, New York

SELECTED TITLES

Close Your Eyes
1978

The Silver Bear
1987

The Pizza Pie Slugger
1989

Pretend You're a Cat
1990

In 1492
1991

*I Spy:
A Book of Picture Riddles*
(first in a series)
1992

*Happy Birthday,
Martin Luther King*
1993

Snow Angel
1995

Sun Song
1995

Home Sweet Home
1997

*I Love You:
A Rebus Poem*
2000

As a child, when Jean Marzollo wasn't playing ball or riding her bike, she was probably off with friends making doll clothes. "We were always making things," Jean fondly recalls. "During the summer we would sit under the trees and sew for hours."

Jean likens her experience making clothes to her current life as a writer. She says, "I never thought about being an author when I was young, but the pleasure I now take in making books is the same pleasure I took as a child making doll clothes. The creative process is essentially the same. First, you think of something you want to make, next you plan how you'll do it, and then you do it."

After graduating from college, Jean first worked as a teacher and then as a freelance writer and editor. In 1972 Jean accepted a job that would change her life. She became the editor of *Let's Find Out*, a magazine for kindergarten children. Over the next 20 years, Jean helped make *Let's Find Out* a fun-filled, award-winning magazine. In doing so, Jean came to understand a lot about how children learn. This knowledge has helped her immeasurably as the author of a dizzying variety of books.

Working on *Let's Find Out*, Jean had to stay up-to-date on children's books. After concluding that there weren't any good books on Christopher Columbus for young children, she decided to write one herself. "I worried about how to do it for a long time," Jean remembers. "Then I realized the perfect solution was to keep going with the rhyme that everybody knows: *In fourteen hundred ninety-two/Columbus sailed the ocean blue*." Beginning with that famous line, she spun off a simple rhyming tale based on Columbus's great adventure and called it *In 1492*.

Like many writers, Jean believes it's important to jot down ideas right away. She ruefully admits, "I learned the hard way that if I don't write my ideas down, I forget them." She saves these ideas—they could be as simple as a

rhyme scribbled on a scrap of paper—and files them into folders. Jean depends on these folders for inspiration. "I can't sit down and say, 'Today I'm going to write a picture book.' When I'm stuck for an idea, I look through the files I keep. I can't make ideas happen. Ideas usually come to me while I'm doing other things."

Hard Work and Good Luck

Over the past decade Jean has enjoyed great success with her best-selling I Spy books. "It's just luck, really," Jean modestly claims. "You can't really tell which books will sell. You just have to follow your heart and do what's next."

> **"I love writing simple, rhyming poetry. I love writing early chapter books and easy-to-read books. And I love writing nonfiction. The truth is, I just love writing."**

The I Spy books grew directly from Jean's days with *Let's Find Out.* Carol Devine Carson and Jean had asked a wonderful photographer, Walter Wick, to shoot some posters for the magazine. The posters turned out beautifully. They were so original, in fact, that two editors at Scholastic urged Walter, Carol, and Jean to collaborate on a book.

Jean explains how the books are made: "First we discuss various possibilities for scenes. Walter then begins his elaborate imaginative process. For most of the pictures, he devises a set using whatever is needed: blocks, toys, scraps of wood, old shelves, a window frame, chicken wire, fabric, pillow stuffing. Next, he carefully places objects into the scene, many of which he hides."

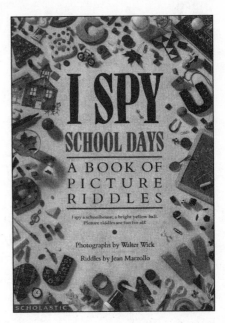

Jean and Walter speak with each other on the phone throughout the photographic process. Looking at test photos, they make sure that there are many objects in each picture—cleverly hidden—that rhyme. Walter then takes the final photo and sends a copy to Jean. With photo in hand, Jean writes the final rhymes.

Jean likes to work on several books at the same time. One week it's a nonfiction biography; the following week she might be working on a book of rhymes. Then the next week (or day!) she might switch to a chapter book for slightly older readers. "That way, if I get stuck," Jean explains, "I can put one project aside and move to another."

DO IT YOURSELF!

Jean Marzollo says: "At a number of schools the children have made their own Pretend You're a Cat books about different animals. Kids can really do a good job of following the patterns." Try it yourself. Read *Pretend You're a Cat* and study it carefully. Now try writing rhymes about your own favorite animals!

Robert McCloskey

Born: September 15, 1914, in Hamilton, Ohio
Home: Scott Islands, Maine

Selected Titles

Lentil
1940

Make Way for Ducklings
(Caldecott Medal)
1941

Homer Price
1943

Blueberries for Sal
(Caldecott Honor Book)
1948

Centerburg Tales
1951

One Morning in Maine
(Caldecott Honor Book)
1952

Time of Wonder
(Caldecott Medal)
1957

*Burt Dow,
Deep-Water Man*
1963

What's the best way to draw a duck? Well, according to Robert McCloskey, author and illustrator of *Make Way for Ducklings*, "You more or less have to think like a duck!" And how, you ask, do you think like a duck? Follow some of them around for a few weeks—at least that's what McCloskey did.

When Robert McCloskey was working on the final sketches for *Make Way for Ducklings*, he began to feel dissatisfied with his drawings. He realized, he says, "I really knew very little about them." So early one morning McCloskey visited a poultry dealer in New York. He told the dealer that he would like to buy some mallards. McCloskey remembers, "I was promptly shown a very noisy shipment that had just come in from the South." That day, Robert McCloskey returned home to his apartment toting four live ducks.

The tiny apartment was pure chaos, filled with flying feathers and waddling, quacking ducks— that, it must be noted, refused to become potty trained. "I spent the next weeks on my hands and knees, armed with a box of Kleenex and a sketchbook, following ducks around the studio and observing them in the bathtub."

As the weeks passed, McCloskey was even able to think like a duck. He says, "No effort is too great to find out as much as possible about the things you're drawing. It's a good feeling to be able to put down a line and know that it is right."

As this story illustrates, McCloskey is something of a perfectionist. If a drawing isn't exactly right, he'll rip it up and start all over. He says, "There are sometimes as many as 20 or 30 drawings before I turn out the one you see in the book— not completed drawings, of course, but ones that explore the best possible way of presenting a particular picture."

A "Serious" Artist

Robert McCloskey grew up in the small town of Hamilton, Ohio. As a child he took piano lessons and learned to play the harmonica, the drums, and the oboe. He had thought that he would become a musician, until he discovered electronics. He loved to tinker with old electric motors and clocks, pulling them apart and trying to put them together again. He even invented a revolving Christmas tree!

> *"Like a musician who likes to have his music listened to, I like to have my pictures looked at and enjoyed."*

Eventually McCloskey decided to become a "serious" artist. "My mind in those days," he recalls, "was filled with odd bits of Greek mythology—Spanish galleons, Oriental dragons, and all the stuff that really and truly great art is made of."

For two summers he lived on Cape Cod and made paintings. But no one bought them. McCloskey confesses, "My career was a bust." Thanks to a conversation with an editor, McCloskey decided to rethink his career. The editor looked at McCloskey's paintings of mythological figures, dragons, and winged horses and gently suggested that he try creating more realistic images. Her comments made him think about growing up in Ohio and the ordinary events of his childhood. Instead of painting fantasies, McCloskey decided to focus on everyday life.

McCloskey's first book, *Lentil*, sprang from his own childhood experiences. His next book was *Make Way for Ducklings*, which is one of the most famous, best-loved books in the history of children's literature. McCloskey first noticed ducklings years earlier when he used to walk through the Boston Public Garden on his way to art school. But at the time, he says, "It never occurred to me to draw those things."

By focusing on ordinary life, Robert McCloskey created many other successful books as well. Several of them were inspired by the experience of living part of each year on an island off the coast of Maine. "Living on an island is lots of fun and lots of work," he says. "In the spring when we first arrive, there are boats to paint, a garden to plant, and a thousand other things to do. But when it's a nice day, we stop our work to go fishing or sailing or picnicking."

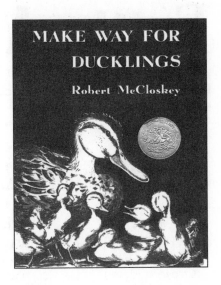

MAKE WAY FOR DUCKLINGS

Robert McCloskey

DO IT YOURSELF!

Robert McCloskey believes that you have to know something very well in order to draw it well. Do you think that's true? Try this experiment. Draw a picture of a cat, using your imagination. Then study a live cat and draw it again. Which picture is better: the first drawing or the second?

Emily Arnold McCully

Born: July 1, 1939, in Galesburg, Illinois
Home: Chatham, New York

As a young girl growing up on Long Island, New York, Emily Arnold McCully was considered, for lack of a better phrase, a tomboy. Indeed, she was an adventurous child who liked to play ball, climb trees, jump fences, and *do stuff*—just like the boys.

Emily was far from the dainty lass who fretted about getting her party dress wrinkled. She recalls the boys of her youth: "I envied their freedom and action-packed lives." The problem was that in those days (and still lingering today), the qualities of courage, strength, and independence were reserved for boys. Girls were supposed to be different, quiet and demure; they were expected to be at home enjoying polite tea parties while the boys were out battling dragons.

It would be accurate to see Emily's recent books as a reaction against those confining stereotypes. Her stories consistently feature strong female characters (not to be confused with tomboys). She depicts girls with courage and strength, grit and determination— girls who *do stuff*.

As an illustrator Emily strives for lively characterization, fast-paced action, and a "just tossed this off"

sense of free-wheeling spontaneity. The artist explains, "My main concern is not trying to make a book look perfect, but for the story to be exciting and clear and for the pictures to have as much life and energy as possible. Those qualities don't usually come from laboring over something over and over and over."

Emily's true breakthrough came when she began to write children's stories of her own. It was nearly 20 years before she successfully achieved it, at age 42. Ironically, Emily's first "authored" book was completely wordless! Emily confesses, "For *Picnic*, I started out with words and an editor pointed out to me that the pictures didn't need words. The story could be told through pictures alone."

It was nevertheless a huge step for

Emily—a step that required an act of bravery. Emily comments, "Part of the courage it takes to be an author—or to do anything worth doing—is to risk rejection and to risk failure." At last she was creating her own books, solely, rather than illustrating the work of others. When Emily began writing, her books took on a more deeply personal tone. Her true voice came bursting forth, unfiltered, uncompromised, and clear. She was finally liberated to explore the things closest to her heart.

> *"Don't worry about what other people are doing. Don't try to emulate. Work from what is inside you, crying out—however softly, however timidly— for expression."*

With more than 200 books behind her ("I really have lost count," Emily admits) perhaps it's simplistic to focus on one character, one book. But *Mirette on the High Wire* provides an ideal prism through which to appreciate the work of Emily Arnold McCully. Emily recalls, "I had just been to Paris for the first time in several years, and that's one of the reasons it's set there. I was excited about Paris all over again. I wanted to write about Paris, and I wanted to write about a brave girl."

Emily reflects, "When I was a child, there were almost no books that interested me that were about girls. I imagine that things have changed now, but people tell me there are not enough stories of adventure and perseverance and daring about girls. And the things I like to write about the most are characters who have goals, who really want to achieve something and realize that it takes hard work as well as courage."

For the character Mirette, Emily drew upon her own feelings for inspiration. She admits, "When I finished that book, one of my friends said to me, 'Oh, this is about you.' I didn't think about that as I was writing it." In *Mirette*, Emily explores many of the major themes that most concern her. Mirette, like an artist, dreams and strives and finally masters a skill—through personal courage and risk. Yet Mirette's story is the perfect metaphor for all achievement: It is the story of a person daring to reach new heights. And it is the story of a female character who possesses the qualities of courage, independence, and inner strength—just like the book's creator.

DO IT YOURSELF!

Emily Arnold McCully is a great believer in taking risks. With each new project she challenges herself to attempt new things. This is how, Emily believes, an artist's work grows and improves. But with challenge and risk also comes failure. Emily confesses, "I am still learning. What I have learned has come from practicing and from making many, many, many, many mistakes." So go ahead . . . try it yourself. Draw something or write something that isn't easy for you. Be brave. Take out a piece of paper and dare to fail. Make mistakes, for they are an essential step on the road to achievement.

Angela Shelf Medearis

Born: November 16, 1956, in Hampton, Virginia
Home: Austin, Texas

SELECTED TITLES

Picking Peas for a Penny
1990

Dancing With the Indians
1991

The Zebra Riding Cowboy
1992

*Dare to Dream:
Coretta Scott King
and the Civil Rights
Movement*
1994

The Singing Man
1994

*The Adventures of
Sugar and Junior*
1995

Poppa's New Pants
1995

The 100th Day of School
1996

*Annie's Gifts
(Feeling Good)*
1997

*The Ghost of
Sifty-Sifty Sam*
1997

Rum-a-Tum-Tum
1997

*Seven Spools of Thread:
A Kwanzaa Story*
2000

The world of children's literature owes a debt of gratitude to a Texas-based law firm. *Really!* Now, surely, lawyers as a group have not contributed much to the field of children's books. But one law firm did—on the day it fired a young, talented woman by the name of Angela Shelf Medearis.

Angela takes up the story from there: "I began writing in October 1987, after I was fired from my job as a legal secretary. Writing was something that had always been in the back of my mind as a way of making money while staying at home," Angela, a self-professed "homebody," explains. "Getting fired was the turning point."

The very day Angela lost her job, she headed directly to the library. Angela dedicated herself over the next few months to researching the publishing industry, studying the craft of writing, and trying to complete a few manuscripts. The words began to pour forth, and the prolific Medearis—a natural, lively storyteller—never looked back.

It may sound like a happy accident that Angela became a writer, but that's not exactly the case. From early childhood, books played an essential role in her life.

Because her father worked for the Air Force, Angela's family was constantly on the move. Angela attended 11 elementary schools, 2 junior high schools, and 3 high schools! Books helped ease the transitions. She says, "I used books and reading as a way of adjusting to new surroundings. I knew that my favorite books would be waiting for me at the library in whatever new place we were going. I also knew that there would be a nice librarian there who would be friendly to me. It made a new school and making new friends much easier to deal with."

Angela also has found support and strength in her uncommonly close family, perhaps drawn even closer by the family's itinerant lifestyle. "My brother [Howard] and sisters [Sandra and Marcy] are my closest friends. When we were children, we loved playing together. We're all grown up now but we still tease each other and act silly together."

"I love writing almost as much as I love my family and chocolate! It makes me feel like a rock star when someone asks for my autograph. Too bad I can't sing!"

Silliness and laughter are a big part of Angela's outgoing personality. In conversation she is dynamic, charming, and ready to laugh aloud. Her humor bubbles forth unexpectedly, as when she jokes about her brother and sisters, "They'll tell you I was a funny, bossy, bratty child, but don't believe it. I was adorable!" One further example: When asked about pets during an online chat, Angela cheerfully explained, "I don't have pets, except a plastic chicken."

"Most people think I'm funny," Angela confesses. "I like to make people laugh. I really, really like to make kids laugh. It's one of the happiest sounds in the world."

Yet Angela has more on her mind than simply getting a laugh. She reflects, "As a child I loved to pretend I was the heroine in fairy tales. The problem was, writers didn't do black girls back then."

Today that's changed. And Angela Shelf Medearis has done a lot to change it. She says, "I write the kind of books I always longed to find in the library when I was a child." This sense of mission—of filling a void in children's literature and reaching out to readers who may have been ignored—drives Angela's work. "I love introducing children all over the world to all the different aspects of African-American history, folklore, and culture," she says. "I love picture books because it's a challenge to convey complex ideas in a simple form for children. I really enjoy factually and vividly presenting history in a 32- or 48-page book. It's wonderful to be able to hold children's attention and teach them something important."

Comfortable with a variety of styles and forms, Angela draws inspiration from family history, historical research, or whatever fancy enters her imaginings. Though Angela has always written with particular attention to the needs of young African Americans, her books—like all great literature—transcend race and color and speak to us all.

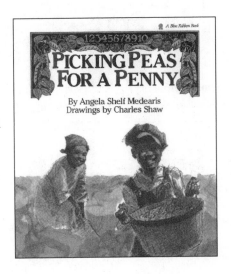

PICKING PEAS FOR A PENNY
By Angela Shelf Medearis
Drawings by Charles Shaw

DO IT YOURSELF!

"Many of my stories are based on my family history," Angela confides. "My first two books, *Picking Peas for a Penny* and *Dancing With the Indians*, are about my mother and her family." Try writing, like Angela, about an event in your own family. It could be a story about a grandparent or a distant relative. Talk to that person, ask questions, and learn about your own family history. Then do everyone a favor and write about it!

Robert Munsch

Born: June 11, 1945, in Pittsburgh, Pennsylvania
Home: Guelph, Ontario, Canada

SELECTED TITLES

The Paper Bag Princess
1980

Murmel, Murmel, Murmel
1982

Thomas' Snowsuit
1985

Love You Forever
1986

Angela's Airplane
1988

A Promise Is a Promise
1988

Giant, or, Waiting for the Thursday Boat
1989

Show and Tell
1991

Alligator Baby
1997

Get Out of Bed!
1998

Aaron's Hair
2000

Although he is a wildly successful author, Robert Munsch claims that he doesn't know a lot about the writing process. That's because he tells his stories aloud. It isn't until after he's told them—in some cases, as many as one hundred times—that Robert finally gets around to putting words to paper. Munsch concedes, "I got into it backwards."

While working in a day-care center for young children, Robert Munsch began telling stories for very practical reasons. He recalls, "I found that I could get kids to shut up at nap time by telling them stories. I worked out this deal where the kids could ask me for one story that I'd already told and I would also make up a new one. At that time I wasn't thinking of being a writer. But the trick was, by letting them ask for only one old story, they only asked for the good ones. The first day-care center where I did that, I made up 519 stories over two years."

Out of those 519 stories, Munsch found that the children requested only about ten of them over and over again. He says, "After two years, I left there with ten good stories."

For Munsch, unlike most writers who sit alone in a room reworking their stories, the revision process comes through repeated tellings. "When I first start telling them," Munsch confides, "they change wildly—whole plots, characters, everything is up for grabs. Once the stories get steady, then it's just little dinky things that change."

But Munsch doesn't think too much about revising and editing. When he's telling his stories, the changes come about naturally. Robert explains, "When I'm performing in front of 40 kids, I'm not thinking like a writer. I'm thinking like a performer. I just want to keep them happy."

You could say that Robert Munsch is a walking, talking, story machine. But where in the world does he get all those ideas? That's a question that Munsch doesn't particularly like. "People are

always asking, 'Where do you get your ideas?'—as if somehow that were the essence. It's not. It's part of the essence. Lots of people have good ideas for books. I have lots of good ideas for books. So what?

> **"Kids either keep laughing, or, if they don't like the story, they get up and leave. That's the honest feedback I depend on."**

"Ideas are cheap; books are expensive. I have no trouble getting ideas. It's books I have trouble getting. There are lots of times when I know I have a good story idea, but it takes me years to actually get a good story. For example, one of my books, *Something Good*, is about going shopping. I'd been trying to do a good shopping story for ten years. I knew the idea was good, but that doesn't necessarily mean a book will happen."

Robert Munsch confesses that it took him a while to learn how to make the transition from storyteller to writer. "At first," he says, "I made the mistake of attempting to change my stories into what I considered to be good writing. They were terrible." Eventually, Munsch figured out that the closer he came to writing his storyteller's version, the better the book would be.

For a story to be worthy of becoming a book, it must first pass a series of Munsch-designed tests. He explains, "When I get a story that's good, I try to drag it through all kinds of situations. My rule's urban/rural: Tell it in the city; tell it in the country. And in Canada, south/north: Tell it in southern Canada and then take it way up into the Arctic. If I can get a story that floats in all those places, it's got to be a pretty good story."

The Paper Bag Princess
STORY • ROBERT N. MUNSCH   ART • MICHAEL MARTCHENKO

Robert Munsch also finds that some of his stories succeed in some places and fail in others. "Sometimes a story isn't publishable simply because it's too tightly woven into one particular community," he says. "I have lots of stories that I've told for Inuit communities up north that work really well in a community where people hunt for a living and eat raw caribou. But they don't work in Toronto because nobody there hunts for a living—and they certainly don't eat raw caribou!"

One thing's for sure: When you pick up a book by Robert Munsch, you can be certain it's been kid-tested and approved!

DO IT YOURSELF!

Robert Munsch says that he makes up most of his stories on the spot. He calls it thinking on his feet. Why not give it a try? Pick a friend and say, "I'm going to make up story about you." And then give it a try.

Mary Pope Osborne

Born: May 20, 1949, in Fort Sill, Oklahoma
Home: New York, New York

SELECTED TITLES

Moonhorse
1988

Favorite Greek Myths
1989

The Many Lives of Benjamin Franklin
1990

American Tall Tales
1991

Dinosaurs Before Dark
(first in the Magic Tree House series)
1992

Mermaid Tales From Around the World
1993

One World, Many Religions
1996

Favorite Medieval Tales
1998

Standing in the Light
(a Dear America book)
1998

Adaline Falling Star
2000

My Secret War
(a Dear America book)
2000

A self-described "professional daydreamer," Mary Pope Osborne possesses a lively, curious mind. To fuel her imagination, Mary is eager to try new things, see new sights, and experience new adventures. It is the story of her life. And it is Mary's life that informs and shapes her stories.

The daughter of an army colonel, Mary moved often as a child. She recalls, "By the time I was 15 I had lived in Oklahoma, Austria, Florida, and four different army posts in Virginia and North Carolina. Moving was never traumatic for me, partly because I had very close and loving relationships with my parents, my twin brother, my younger brother, and my older sister."

Mary adapted easily to living in new places; staying in one place was the problem! "When my dad finally retired to a small town in North Carolina, I nearly went crazy with boredom," Mary says. "I craved the adventure and changing scenery of our military life."

As a teenager Mary discovered the local community theater. An outlet for her passion for pretending, the theater became Mary's joy and salvation. She remembers fondly, "I spent nearly every waking hour after school there, either acting or working backstage. When I stepped from the sunny street into that musty-smelling, dark little theater, all things seemed possible."

While studying drama and comparative religions in college, Mary became fascinated by fairy tales, mythology, and history. The stories stirred her imagination and made her long to visit far-flung lands—which is exactly what she did after college, traveling to countries such as Iraq, Iran, Afghanistan, Pakistan, and India. After returning to the United States, Mary eventually met her future husband, Will Osborne, moved to New York, and married in 1976.

One day, seemingly out of the blue, Mary began to write a novel for young adults based on her childhood experiences. It was a serious, realistic novel titled *Run, Run as Fast as You Can*. Says Mary, "Finally, I knew what I wanted to be when I grew up."

> **"Once you get something down on paper, the fun really starts. Because then you can take what you've got and make it better."**

Today Mary has published a sweeping variety of books for children, addressing most of her lifetime passions. Her books have touched upon world mythology, different religions, distant cultures, and pure fantasy. Yet most readers know Mary best for her popular Magic Tree House series.

In this acclaimed series, all of Mary's skills and interests come together. She writes of dinosaurs and mummies, pirates and Vikings, while taking readers on wild, magical trips to far-off places such as the rain forest, a coral reef, the Wild West, and even the moon. The writer's world is limitless— just the way Mary likes it.

Mary describes writing as a combination of joy and hard work. From the beginning, she knew that she wanted the Magic Tree House series to include time travel. She confesses, "I thought it would be pretty boring unless I could find a way to make it different from book to book."

Like most good writing, the series didn't come easily at first. "It took forever to invent that little universe," laughs Mary. "At first I tried a magic museum. I tried a magic cellar. I tried a magic artist's studio in the woods. There were a few points where I almost gave up." Mary credits her editor, Mallory Loehr, for providing encouragement and insight. "It was almost essential that this young woman help me sort out my ideas," Mary explains gratefully.

According to Mary, the Magic Tree House series owes much of its success to the contributions of children. "All of the books have been steered by the interests of kids," she claims. "The contact I've had with children has brought over-whelming joy into my life. I love the letters I get, and I love reading the countless Magic Tree House stories that they've written. I feel as if these kids and I are all exploring the creative process together, using our imaginations, plus our reading and writing skills, to take us where we want to go. This, I tell my small fellow authors, is *true* magic."

FAVORITE
MEDIEVAL TALES
MARY POPE OSBORNE ❦ TROY HOWELL

DO IT YOURSELF!

Mary Pope Osborne enjoys revising her work, sometimes rewriting a story as many as 30 times! "I find it a really exciting process," she explains. "Making a few words live is so much more interesting to me than having long, dull sentences." Why not try it yourself? Write a sentence. Then step back, take a long look at it, and try to make it better. Then do it again and again, until it's the best you can make it. Says Mary, "Rewriting is a lot of fun!"

AUTHOR

Barbara Park

Born: April 21, 1947, in Mount Holly, New Jersey
Home: Paradise Valley, Arizona

SELECTED TITLES

Skinnybones
1982

The Kid in the Red Jacket
1987

My Mother Got Married (and Other Disasters)
1989

Maxie, Rosie, and Earl—Partners in Grime
1990

Rosie Swanson: Fourth-Grade Geek for President
1991

Junie B. Jones and the Stupid Smelly Bus (first in a series)
1992

Mick Harte Was Here
1995

The Graduation of Jake Moon
2000

Best-selling author Barbara Park did not take the usual path to becoming a writer. "As a kid, I didn't even read much," Barbara confesses. "I bought books from the school book club because I liked the smell of them. It was nice to have this pile of new books. But I really had no great desire to read them!"

Barbara was a lively, active child with a motormouth and a sharp sense of humor. She had a great many interests, but writing was not one of them. "To me, writing was an assignment, period. I was not particularly imaginative. I didn't sit around and make up stories to entertain my friends. But I was always the class clown. In high school I was voted 'Wittiest,' which, let's be honest, is just a nice way of saying 'Goofy!'"

It wasn't until after college, marriage, and the birth of two children, that Barbara began to think seriously about writing. "I wanted to see if I could put my sense of humor to work. Because, sad to say, it was the only thing for which I'd ever got any recognition. I thought, Maybe I can write funny."

Working at home while her two boys were in school, Barbara concentrated on books for middle-grade readers. Barbara lists *The Kid in the Red Jacket, My Mother Got Married (and Other Disasters),* and *Mick Harte Was Here* as personal favorites. She considers her best work to be *Mick Harte Was Here.* Many readers agree. In a stunning achievement, Barbara addresses a boy's tragic, accidental death, with writing that is at once deeply heartfelt and—amazingly—joyously funny.

In all of her books, no matter the seriousness of the theme, Barbara's humor spontaneously bubbles to the surface. In fact, Barbara has made something of a career out of focusing on funny, irreverent, wisecracking kids who, like her, just can't walk away from a punch line.

Though Barbara's books are moral in the truest sense of the word,

she steers clear of heavy messages and "life lessons." Says Barbara, "I happen to think that a book is of extraordinary value if it gives the reader nothing more than a smile or two. It's perfectly okay to take a book, read it, have a good time, giggle and laugh—and turn off the TV. I love that."

> **"If you're lucky, there are lots of things about being a kid that can stick with you forever. And I for one wouldn't have it any other way."**

In the early 1990s, Barbara was approached by Random House with the idea of writing a series for younger readers. It scared her half to death. Barbara admits, "There was some question as to whether or not my dry sense of humor would be picked up by younger kids."

In the end Barbara decided that she'd have to write to please herself, to be true to her own sensibilities. "I can't change my sense of humor," Barbara explains. "If I did, it wouldn't even be me trying to write this book. It would be me trying to write like somebody who didn't think like me!"

Barbara soon created the irrepressible character Junie B. Jones. This best-selling children's character, who all-too-often said and did all the wrong things, elbowed her way into the spotlight. Barbara didn't have to look far for inspiration. "Junie B. is me in an exaggerated form," Barbara admits. "I think the core of most of my characters is me. I mean, where else is it going to come from? It's got to be from you."

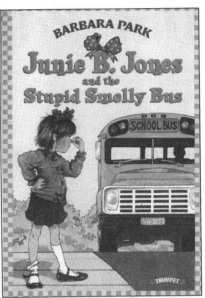

Though Junie B. is in kindergarten (with a move to first grade coming soon), Barbara has an uncanny knack for inhabiting her world. She says, "I've never had a problem becoming five years old in my head. I really think that you basically stay the same person all your life. I feel the essence of me hasn't changed."

Junie B. is by no means perfect. She acts out in class, she's not always respectful, and she tends to massacre the English language whenever she opens her mouth (which is often). An ideal role model? Forget about it. Junie B. is much more than that— with her foibles and mistakes, she is as genuine as her readers. Junie B. is a pretty terrific kid doing her best to get it right— and happily succeeding most of the time.

DO IT YOURSELF!

Kids often write to Barbara with ideas for new Junie B. adventures. Barbara is grateful for the help, since she finds coming up with "the nuts and bolts of the story," or the plot, the hardest part of writing. Try to think of your own Junie B. story. It could be something that happened in your life. But this time, make Junie B. the character—what happens next?

Dav Pilkey

Born: March 4, 1966, in Cleveland, Ohio
Home: Eugene, Oregon

SELECTED TITLES

Dav Pilkey (pronounced "Dave" and, well, "Pilkey") has been trying to make kids laugh for as long as he can remember. "I was the class clown," Dav admits, "and I was constantly getting in trouble for making other kids laugh."

Today, making kids laugh is pretty much Dav's full-time job. As a children's book author and illustrator, he has become what can only be described as a professional class clown. Dav's books are loved by millions of kids everywhere. And—to his great satisfaction—Dav *still* manages to annoy the occasional "humor-challenged" adult.

It all started in grade school. Dav recalls, "I could make wonderful noises by pressing my hands into my face and blowing really hard. I held the classroom record for the number of crayons I could stick up my nose at one time. And I was also quite talented at playing songs on my armpit."

This outrageous behavior did not endear Dav to his teachers. "When I was in second grade, I got in trouble a lot. To punish me, my teacher would send me out into the hallway. Before long, I was spending so much time in the hall that my teacher moved a desk out there for me."

Dav seized the opportunity by stuffing the desk with art supplies and paper. To keep himself busy, he drew pictures and made up stories. Dav didn't realize it then, but he was preparing himself for his future career. "I used to staple sheets of paper together and write my own comic books," he remembers. "I had invented a whole slew of amazing superheroes, including Captain Underpants, who flew around the city in his underwear giving wedgies to all the bad guys."

Dav continues, "These comic books were a real hit with my classmates; however, they weren't too popular with my teachers. I remember one teacher who, after furiously ripping up one of my stories, told me I'd better start taking life a little more seriously because I couldn't spend the rest of my days making silly books."

Boy, was she wrong.

Still, it wasn't all spitballs, wedgies, and chuckles for young Dav. "I had a pretty tough time in school," he recalls. "I had reading problems, and I didn't learn the same way that most of the kids in my class learned. I was discouraged a lot, and sometimes I felt like a total failure. But I had a lot of encouragement and support from my parents. They helped me get through the hard times."

"I think my books are pretty funny, so I'm not surprised that kids like them, too. I guess what surprises me is that a guy like me got to have such a cool job."

Surprisingly, Dav's second-grade teacher—the same one who often pointed to the door and hollered, "PILKEY, OUT!"—provided the inspiration for Captain Underpants. "She used the word *underpants* during class one day, and everybody laughed," Dav recalls. "She got mad and said, 'Underwear is not funny!' This only made us laugh harder. At that moment I discovered that underwear was a powerful thing: It could make my friends laugh."

In college at Kent State University, one of Dav's teachers encouraged him to try his hand at children's books. Finally he found the perfect vehicle for his bursting energy and talent. A self-taught artist, Dav learned how to write by reading his favorite books over and over again. Those books included the George and Martha series, by James Marshall; the Stupids books, by Harry Allard; and the Frog and Toad books, by Arnold Lobel.

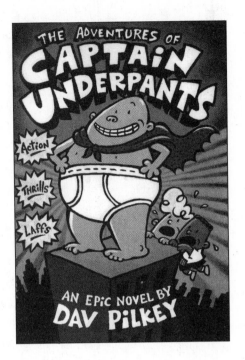

In 1997 Dav's beloved character, Captain Underpants ("fighting for Truth, Justice, and all that is Pre-Shrunk and Cottony"), finally got published. It was an instant, runaway best-seller. Dav doesn't seem much changed by his success. He lives simply, close to nature, and makes sure to give himself plenty of time for daydreaming. Dav reflects, "If my books can help kids get excited about writing and reading, that is great, but that really isn't what I was after. Really, I just wanted to make them laugh."

DO IT YOURSELF!

"I never try to 'think up' a story," claims Dav Pilkey. "I live a very simple life, and often spend a few hours each day just daydreaming. It is usually during these times that my ideas come to me." In a nutshell, that's Dav's advice to kids. He urges, "Spend as much time as you can daydreaming." So give it a try. Put down the pen. Put away the paper. Close your eyes—and let your imagination wander. You may be surprised where it ends up!

J. Brian Pinkney

Born: August 28, 1961, in Boston, Massachusetts
Home: Brooklyn, New York

SELECTED TITLES

The Boy and the Ghost
1989

The Ballad of Belle Dorcas
1990

Sukey and the Mermaid
1992

Happy Birthday, Martin Luther King
1993

Max Found Two Sticks
1994

The Faithful Friend
(Caldecott Honor Book)
1995

The Adventures of Sparrowboy
1997

Watch Me Dance
1997

Duke Ellington: The Piano Prince and His Orchestra
(Caldecott Honor Book)
1998

Cosmo and the Robot
2000

If Brian's last name sounds familiar, it may be because you've heard of his dad, Jerry Pinkney, the award-winning illustrator of such books as *The Patchwork Quilt, Mirandy and Brother Wind,* and *The Talking Eggs.* Brian cheerfully admits to following in his father's footsteps. "When I was growing up," Brian says, "my father did a lot of advertising and editorial work as well as books. Because my father was an artist, I wanted to be like him. He was my idol."

Brian is glad to have a father who can give him advice about creating art. "There's no competition between us," Brian states. "It's a friendship. That's probably because he is such a nice guy. He never tried to tell me, 'This is how you make pictures.' He was always very supportive of whatever I did."

As an African-American artist in a field that has been dominated by white illustrators, Brian brings an added sense of responsibility to his work. "For me," he explains, "the whole push for multicultural literature is an effort to compensate for all the years of not focusing on the contributions of other ethnic groups to America." Yet Brian points out that he's only doing what's natural for him. "It's kind of like a writer who writes from his own experiences," Brian says. "I'm illustrating out of my own experiences and my own heritage—it's like I'm covering thousands of years in terms of a black culture that hasn't really been expressed. Besides," he adds, "my work is so personal, I feel like I'm doing books about me."

As a child Brian attended mostly white schools. He jokes, "I went to integrated schools—but they weren't integrated until I got there!" At home Brian's family made sure to celebrate their cultural background. But school was a different world: "In school I was black and the rest of the world was white," he recalls. "We spent about one week on black history. I was so self-conscious during that one week because everything was directed to me, or at least I felt that way. So by doing books like *The Ballad of Belle Dorcas*, it's my chance to catch up on my own heritage."

"I've always been very goal oriented. But now I'm just going to follow my art—wherever that takes me, that's fine."

Another book that holds special meaning for Brian is *Happy Birthday, Martin Luther King* by Jean Marzollo. Brian says, "I went down to Atlanta and visited the actual house in which he was born. I wanted to keep the book simple, but at the same time I wanted it to be monumental in feeling." To achieve this, Brian drew the illustrations so that readers are always looking up at the figures in the book.

"My generation is the generation that came right after the civil rights movement," Brian explains. "A lot of opportunities I've had were because of Martin Luther King's work. He opened up so many doors for me and for so many other children."

In many of his books, Brian uses an illustrative technique called scratchboard. Brain describes how he discovered this unique approach: "When I was doing my

first picture book, *The Boy and the Ghost*, I decided that the way I was doing my artwork wasn't satisfying to me. I was feeling that I wanted something else out of my artwork, but I didn't know what it was."

At the advice of a teacher, Brian began to experiment with the scratchboard process. "I fell in love with it," he says. Working on scratchboard offers a sense of rhythm that pleases Brian, who professes to be a drum enthusiast. "There's always sound when I'm scratching. I lay down the lines in patterns. It's like doing a drumroll. You can't think about how many times the sticks hit the drum. It's like: *ch-ch, ch-ch, ch-ch*. When I'm scratching, I often play music in the background. I'm just putting down rhythm. I like the sound it makes; it's part of the whole process."

by Jean Marzollo • Illustrated by J. Brian Pinkney

SCHOLASTIC

DO IT YOURSELF!

Study the illustrations in Brian's books (*The Ballad of Belle Dorcas* and *Sukey and the Mermaid* provide fine examples). Now try your own scratchboard illustrations—all you need are paper, a black crayon, and an artist's knife. Just put a layer of black crayon on a sheet of paper and scratch into it. If you'd like to try Brian's technique, get a piece of white illustration board and cover it with black ink. After the ink dries, scratch into it with the knife. "There are also two scratchboard nibs you can buy in an art supply store," Brian adds. "One looks like an arrowhead and the other looks like a spoon."

Jerry Pinkney

Born: December 22, 1939, in Philadelphia, Pennsylvania
Home: Croton-on-Hudson, New York

SELECTED TITLES

*The Adventures of Spider:
West African Folktales*
1964

*Apples on a Stick: The
Folklore of Black Children*
1983

The Patchwork Quilt
1985

The Uncle Remus Tales
1987

Mirandy and Brother Wind
(Caldecott Honor Book)
1988

The Talking Eggs
(Caldecott Honor Book)
1989

Turtle in July
1989

John Henry
(Caldecott Honor Book)
1994

*Minty: A Story of Young
Harriet Tubman*
1996

Rikki-Tikki-Tavi
1997

The Little Match Girl
1999

Aesop's Fables
2000

"A successful illustration," states artist Jerry Pinkney with absolute certainty, "starts with a good manuscript."

Judging from the success of Jerry's illustrations, he's worked on some very fine manuscripts indeed. "I've been very fortunate," Jerry says. "Actually, it's amazing! Because with my success, I'm now getting even better manuscripts to work from."

Almost every day, Jerry receives a new manuscript in the mail. It's difficult to decide which ones to illustrate. For Jerry, first and foremost, the manuscript must reach him on an emotional level. Jerry explains, "I'm looking, first of all, for an exciting story to work on. At that point, it really has nothing to do with whether it's a good story, in terms of how well it's written. I'm only responding to it in terms of illustrations. Only after the second or third go-round do I begin to think, Hey, this story is really well written!"

The manuscript must please Jerry in a variety of ways. Jerry says, "I ask myself, Is there really a good, strong reason to do the book? Is there really a chance to do something that's important to me? Certainly in the case of

African-American stories, I'm drawn to them because there's such a need for those books. But that's also true of a story that might be about a Spanish kid, or a story about Native Americans. Then there's always one last thing to consider," Jerry says with a laugh. "Whether the project can fit into my crazy schedule."

Thinking on Paper

Jerry Pinkney uses drawing as a way to see his ideas. It's as if he doesn't know exactly what he thinks until the pencil hits the paper. Jerry tries to explain, "I don't see things until I draw them. When I put a line down, the only thing I know is how it

should feel, and I know when it doesn't feel right.

"I'm not one who sits right down and does a lot of sketching at first. I work best by thinking about an assignment for awhile, jotting down notes as ideas come to me. Then I do a few rough thumbnail sketches. These sketches help me figure out correct composition and how to set up situations."

During the early stages of Jerry's creative process, he "wallows in reference material." That's because Jerry likes to makes his drawings as true-to-life as possible. Jerry points out, "If you look at the books, the clothing and setting are very researched. I try to set my stories in a specific time and place. In a way, it's like theater. I'm trying to build a set for these characters."

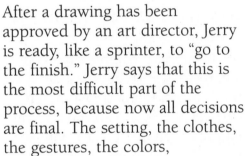

"My work has allowed me to dream."

If Jerry Pinkney's characters look lifelike to you, it's because he often asks live models to act out the story while he takes photographs. Then he uses the photographs when he draws the final illustrations.

"The models I choose help bring out my characters' inner life. When I find a model that has the physical attributes I want in a character, I pose and direct him or her in ways that pull out the character I'm looking for. When I work with models that happen to be children, I have them read the manuscript. Then we act the story out together."

Jerry Pinkney feels that models are essential to his particular style of working. "My work is fairly realistic," he says. "Gestures of the hands, for example, cannot just come out of my head. I really need that figure responding in front of me."

After a drawing has been approved by an art director, Jerry is ready, like a sprinter, to "go to the finish." Jerry says that this is the most difficult part of the process, because now all decisions are final. The setting, the clothes, the gestures, the colors, the style—every detail must be exactly right. It's very difficult work. But there are magical times when everything goes perfectly. "If that particular painting gives back what you have in your head, then it's magical," Jerry Pinkney says. "There are times when pictures sort of take off on their own. Illustrating books can be a wonderful experience!"

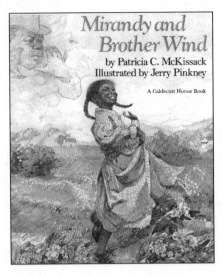

Mirandy and Brother Wind
by Patricia C. McKissack
Illustrated by Jerry Pinkney

A Caldecott Honor Book

DO IT YOURSELF!

The Canadian goose is Jerry Pinkney's favorite illustration from *Turtle in July*. For Jerry, the struggle was to make the goose seem alive. He solved the problem by drawing the goose with its leg lifted up and its neck twisted around. Make your own animal drawing. But, like Jerry Pinkney, be sure to give it some gesture or movement that makes it come alive!

Patricia Polacco

Born: July 11, 1944, in Lansing, Michigan
Home: Oakland, California

SELECTED TITLES

Meteor!
1987

The Keeping Quilt
1988

Rechenka's Eggs
1988

Babushka's Doll
1990

Just Plain Fancy
1990

Thunder Cake
1990

Chicken Sunday
1992

Mrs. Katz and Tush
1992

The Bee Tree
1993

Pink and Say
1994

Mrs. Mack
1998

The Butterfly
2000

Patricia Polacco grew up listening to the wonderful stories of her parents and grandparents, her head swimming with images and characters. "My fondest memories," she recalls, "are of sitting around a stove or open fire, eating apples and popping corn while listening to the old ones [her grandparents] tell glorious stories about the past."

Patricia was born in Lansing, Michigan. Her parents divorced when she was three years old and her brother, Richard, was seven. Patricia recalls, "Even though my parents lived apart, they both were very involved in our lives. We spent the school year with my mother and her parents on a small farm in Union City, Michigan, and the summers with my father in Williamston, Michigan."

In Patricia Polacco's books, as in her life, family roots are important. "The old ones" provided most of the inspiration for her stories. Patricia says, "Babushka [Grandma] and her family came from the Ukraine, just outside of Kiev in Russia. My Diadushka [Grandpa] came from Soviet Georgia. My mother's parents were great historians, but they also took us to the world of fancy and magic

with stories. People on both sides of my family saw perfectly ordinary events as miraculous. And without this appreciation of even the smallest, tenderest little thing, you're doomed."

"When I'm home I'm usually in sweats and gym shoes, my hair barely combed, and I'll be drenched with perspiration after sitting and thinking."

As a writer and illustrator, Patricia brings this same sense of appreciation to her books. She's equally comfortable weaving a colorful yarn based upon her Russian heritage as she is retelling an event from her childhood. Her stories are rich in cultural detail and

filled with characters of different ages, races, and religions. And always there is a deep pleasure in the simplest things. "You have to look for the miracles in very ordinary events," insists Patricia.

At the age of seven, Patricia moved with her mother to Oakland, California, and returned to Michigan each summer to spend time with her father. Filled with a diverse array of people, Oakland was an exciting place for young Patricia. She still lives there. With obvious pride, Patricia describes her neighborhood: "We live in an urban mixed neighborhood, which means that my neighbors come in as many colors, ideas, and belief systems as there are people on this planet."

Patricia derives great satisfaction from seeing different cultures come together in mutual understanding. "Instead of separating and pulling apart, we should be uniting and pulling together," she says. This theme is sounded again and again in her stories.

Rock Around the Clock

Early each morning, dressed in a sweat suit, Patricia will sit in a rocking chair and rock rhythmically, back and forth. This is her time—a time for gathering energy, thoughts, and dreams. Patricia says of her daily habit: "I had a wonderful childhood, but the only pain I had was out of my inability to do schoolwork easily. I have dyslexia and dysnumeria. In my

The Keeping Quilt
Patricia Polacco

dreams, of course, I was perfect. Rocking was something that I did that made me feel whole. And it has carried over into my adult life. My husband and kids could tell you—there are a couple of hours in the morning and sometimes in the evening when I just need to rock.

"When I am composing a story, I sit in one of my rocking chairs and dream it up. For me, rocking is important to the process. I have 12 rocking chairs in the house, and I keep pens and small pads next to them, in case a real good idea springs into my head."

According to Patricia, the most important aspect of storytelling is to write with honest emotions. She advises: "Write about things that you really experience! When the story has a great deal of meaning for you, it very probably will have meaning for others as well."

Patricia's success has given her the opportunity to visit with children in schools across the country. She says, "That's the whole reason for doing this work. If I couldn't be around children, there would almost be no point."

DO IT YOURSELF!

Patricia tells how she got the idea for *The Keeping Quilt*: "One day I took out our quilt and said, 'I want to draw every situation in our family that this quilt has been witness to.' So I drew them and that's how the book began." Try it yourself. Think of an item in your house—perhaps a mirror or an old stuffed chair—and draw pictures of different scenes in your family history that it has witnessed.

Jack Prelutsky

Born: September 8, 1940, in Brooklyn, New York
Home: Mercer Island, Washington

SELECTED TITLES

The Headless Horseman Rides Tonight
1980

Rolling Harvey Down the Hill
1980

The Baby Uggs Are Hatching
1982

It's Snowing! It's Snowing!
1984

The New Kid on the Block
1984

Tyrannosaurus Was a Beast: Dinosaur Poems
1988

Something Big Has Been Here
1990

The Dragons Are Singing Tonight
1993

Monday's Troll
1996

The Gargoyle on the Roof
1999

It's Raining Pigs & Noodles
2000

Poet Jack Prelutsky confesses, "I'm a compulsive note-taker. I always have a notebook with me because I'm always seeing things. The most frequently asked question is always, 'How do you get your ideas?' I find it impossible NOT to have ideas! I have ideas because I'm alive. As long as I keep my senses alert and remain open to the world, the ideas continue to flow."

Jack admits, "I don't know ahead of time which of my notes are going to turn into a poem. A note can be anything. It can be a funny name, a joke, something I overheard, an idea that popped into my mind, a rhyme, an idea for a new game—there are no rules. My only rule is: Write it down immediately. Because if I don't, I'll forget it."

Jack works only when he's inspired. "I can go for days, even months, without writing at all," the poet confesses. "There are times when I have no more need to write than the butcher or the guy next door. But one day I will wake up and sort of say, 'Today.' Then I do a complete turnaround. I become obsessed with writing. I write around the clock. I live in my pajamas. I become an

impossible person. I work and work, 16 or 18 hours in a row. I'll do this for weeks at a time."

At First, Poetry Was Boring

As a boy growing up in the Bronx, New York, Jack found that poetry—or at least the poetry he was taught in school—was a lot like liver. "I simply couldn't stand the stuff," Jack says with distaste. "I was told that it was good for me, but I wasn't convinced."

The problem was, the teachers in school only taught very old poetry that was written by, well, dead people. Jack stresses that he has nothing against dead people—"I don't blame them," Jack says. "It's not their fault they're dead." It was just that the poems had nothing to do with his everyday life.

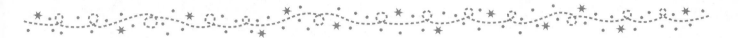

Jack wondered why there couldn't be other types of poems. "It would have been nice to hear poems I related to, such as poems about people like myself or things that I enjoyed—sports, dinosaurs, dragons, the things kids think about."

"I sing poems, I jump up and down, I use props, anything that will help make it come alive. The thing is, it's not boring. Poetry is fun."

Sitting in his studio, a room crammed with literally thousands of poetry books for children, Jack often starts the writing day with a few warm-up exercises. Like an athlete stretching before a game, he limbers up his mind before writing. He plays word games on his computer. He fills in a crossword puzzle. He makes up a list of silly, ridiculous names. It gets his creative juices flowing.

Because he is asked the question so often, Jack makes a great effort to explain, honestly and sincerely, where his ideas come from. "Everything I see or hear can become a poem," Jack offers. "When I was a kid, there was a worm-eating contest in my neighborhood. That became a poem called 'Willie Ate a Worm,' which appears in *Rolling Harvey Down the Hill*. I ate in a diner that had awful food. This became 'Gussie's Greasy Spoon' in *The New Kid on the Block*."

It's fascinating to hear Jack give a detailed description of his creative process. Here's how one poem got started: "I was in the market buying some boneless breasts of chicken and I suddenly asked myself, 'What about the rest of the chicken? Was that boneless too?' All right, so now I take out my notebook and write it down: *boneless chicken. Think about it.* So now I take the idea: Yes, there is such a thing as a boneless chicken. I don't have to make up any more silly things, because all I have to do is pretend I'm a reporter and ask that boneless chicken some basic questions, such as who, why, what, where, when, what if, and why not. For example, I wondered what sort of egg a boneless chicken would lay. First I thought, a boneless egg. But eggs are boneless, so that's not funny. Then one day I was having scrambled eggs for breakfast. There it was, the ending for my poem!"

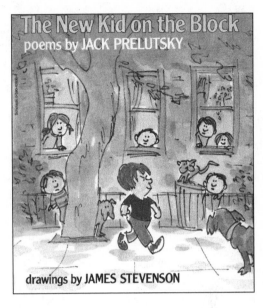

The New Kid on the Block
poems by JACK PRELUTSKY

drawings by JAMES STEVENSON

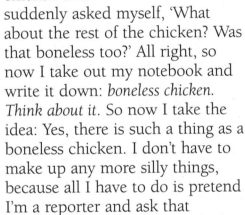

DO IT YOURSELF!

Jack Prelutsky thinks that poetry can be fun. More than fun, it should be a rip-roaring good time. So why not throw a poetry party. Here's Jack's idea: "Have a Something Big party. Children can dress up in oversized clothing, such as novelty eyeglasses, huge neckties, hats, and shoes, and bring in oversized cookies and other big foods for refreshments."

Barbara Reid

Born: November 16, 1957, in Toronto, Ontario, Canada
Home: Toronto, Ontario, Canada

SELECTED TITLES

The New Baby Calf
1984

Have You Seen Birds?
1987

Playing With Plasticine
1988

Sing a Song of
Mother Goose
1988

Effie
1990

Two by Two
1993

Gifts
1995

The Party
1997

Fun With Modeling Clay
1998

Golden Goose
2000

According to Barbara Reid, coming up with the idea for an illustration can take anywhere from five minutes to five weeks. She explains, "With some pages I know from the beginning exactly what I want to do. With other pages I can walk around for days accomplishing nothing. It's really frustrating. I clean the house, I shop, I reorganize cupboards. I do all kinds of stuff just to avoid dealing with it. Then an idea comes somehow.

"When I visit kids," Barbara says, "I try to give them an idea of what it's like to be an illustrator. It seems easy if you look at someone's finished illustrations. But if you read the manuscript on a bare, typewritten page, then you realize what an illustrator has to do to help bring a story to life."

When Barbara is searching for the right way to illustrate a manuscript, she'll often surround herself with pictures, clippings, and reference books. It's as if she's preparing the house for an invited guest—in this case, an idea— to come visit. Barbara explains, "I just lay out all the possibilities for an idea to come in, and then I wait."

Playing With Plasticine

Readers first began to appreciate Barbara's talent with the publication of *The New Baby Calf*. In it, Barbara selected an unusual technique to create the pictures: She used plasticine, basically the same stuff that many kids play with in preschool.

Barbara thinks that with a little effort, just about anybody can create a good picture using plasticine. "Plasticine is friendly," she says with a laugh. "You can watch the most serious people in the world sit down at a table and slowly they'll start twiddling with it. Suddenly they are having a great time, very involved in making a dinosaur. It's like ice cream: everybody likes it."

Barbara also enjoys working with plasticine because it never completely hardens. This allows

her to keep adding bits and pieces to her pictures. She describes the process: "I'll look at an illustration, and at the last minute I'll stick on a bug or something because the picture seems to need it. That's the really fun part. Sometimes it ends up being one of the most important parts of the picture because it gives the illustration that little kick."

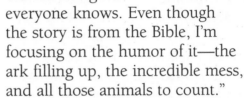

"I'm doing the same thing now that I've done since I was four. I read a story and then make a picture of it. I've been lucky."

When choosing a project, Barbara is attracted to new challenges, new ways to grow as an artist. She says, "I guess I get interested if it's something I haven't done before. I don't like to be repetitive."

After illustrating *Have You Seen Birds?* Barbara tried her hand at nursery rhymes with *Sing a Song of Mother Goose*. She enjoyed the change. "I'd never had a chance to illustrate costumes before," she says. "Birds and calves are dressed as they're dressed, and you can't play around with it. With *Mother Goose*, I worked in all kinds of colors. It's so much more exciting to do faces than beaks."

Next, Barbara accepted another challenge: writing her first picture book. She said in an interview at

the time, "I'm working on a story about Noah's Ark right now. I like doing traditional things. It's a fun challenge, taking something that is well known and interpreting it. As a basis for the text, I'm using an old folk song that everyone knows. Even though the story is from the Bible, I'm focusing on the humor of it—the ark filling up, the incredible mess, and all those animals to count."

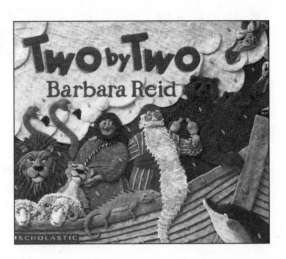

Barbara has deep respect for the words in a story. She says, "You see some books that have been around for a million years with crummy illustrations. But it's the story that people keep coming back to." She adds, firmly, "The story is the most important part."

Since Barbara Reid doesn't usually write her own books, she must choose her stories from among the manuscripts sent to her by editors. Barbara confesses, "It's a big responsibility. I don't want to do any old book. I want to do something really good, and I don't always know how to find it. That's my dream, to find that wonderful story."

DO IT YOURSELF!

Barbara Reid is impressed by the creativity of many children. She says, "I've seen some incredible work by kids who use *Have You Seen Birds?* as a model to create their own books. Instead of birds, they'll use pirates, bugs, even dinosaurs. They imitate the rhythms of the verse and do the illustrations themselves. It's really neat." Why not try it?

Faith Ringgold

Born: October 8, 1930, in Harlem, New York
Home: Harlem, New York

SELECTED TITLES

Tar Beach
(Caldecott Honor Book)
1991

*Aunt Harriet's
Underground Railroad
in the Sky*
1992

*Dinner at Aunt
Connie's House*
1993

*My Dream of
Martin Luther King*
1995

Bonjour, Lonnie
1996

Talking to Faith Ringgold
1996

*If a Bus Could Talk:
The Story of Rosa Parks*
1999

The Invisible Princess
1999

To hear Faith Ringgold tell it, she had a storybook childhood. Faith describes growing up in Harlem, New York, during the 1930s with infectious enthusiasm: "My childhood was magical," she says. "I had a great time. Mother took me to see the great performers of the time—Billie Holiday and Duke Ellington, among others—and to museums and public landmarks like the Statue of Liberty. She put me in touch with the best."

In her family Faith was the youngest, with an older brother and sister. Her parents were hardworking people, determined to provide their children with a positive environment and a quality education. Faith was fortunate. Even during the Great Depression, her father managed to hold a job and keep food on the table. Faith clearly remembers childhood friends who didn't have it so easy. "I still remember the day I was tripping home from school with a friend. We walked by some household belongings piled in the street and my friend said, 'That's my doll! These are my things!' Her family had been evicted."

Thinking back to that time, Faith

pointedly adds: "Neighbors took them in. That's what we did in those days. We took care of our friends. We didn't leave them homeless in the street."

From an early age, Faith benefited from two family traditions that would help shape her career as an artist. First, there was storytelling: "Everyone was a storyteller when I was a child," Faith says. "The stories told to me when I was a little girl weren't folktales. They were real tales about real people's lives. Our families wanted to tell us what life was really like, what it took to survive."

The next important tradition was sewing. "My mother was a dressmaker and fashion designer. She taught me to sew and to love fabrics. She learned to sew from her mother, who in turn learned from her mother, and so on, back to my great-great-grandmother, Susie Shannon, who was a slave.

She worked making quilts for the plantation owners."

"My fondest memories of growing up in Harlem are the people. People on my street, people in my building, friends of mine I saw every day."

Bursting with a desire to express herself through art, Faith was determined to become an artist. She graduated from the City College of New York in 1950. To make ends meet, she taught art in the New York City public schools from 1955 to 1973. During that time, Faith continued to produce new and exciting artwork. "I always saw myself as an artist who taught art," she reflects. "That's the point of being an artist. You can communicate things that you feel and see. You are a voice. That is a very powerful thing."

Story Quilts

Faith began experimenting with a new art form called story quilts, works that combine painting, sewing with different fabrics, and storytelling. A story quilt looks like an ordinary patchwork quilt. It is made in the traditional way, with patches of cloth sewn together. But Faith added some panels with words and others with illustrations. In a way they were like picture books on blankets!

Faith says, "I never knew until 1989 that I would—or could— write and illustrate children's books. Andrea Cascardi, who was an editor at Crown publishers at the time, called me to say she had seen a poster of my painted story quilt 'Tar Beach.' She had read the story on the quilt and thought it would make a good children's book."

To create *Tar Beach*, Faith drew upon her childhood experiences—and wrote what was in her heart. She remembered how, for her apartment-dwelling family, going up on the black asphalt roof had been as much fun as going to the beach. Faith recalls, "My father would come home from work and take the mattress up for us, my mother would fix our bed, and all of us kids would get a chance to sleep together on the one mattress." During those times, refreshed by cool breezes and stirred by the glorious vision of the city at night, Faith was filled with a magical feeling. "When you got up on the roof," Faith says, "you could see everything. The whole world was open to you. It was just totally special."

DO IT YOURSELF!

Can you fly? Faith Ringgold says you can—all you need is a little imagination! Sit down with a pen and paper and try to describe what it might feel like to fly. Where would you go? What would you see? Go on, close your eyes . . . and dream away.

113

Joanne Ryder

Born: September 16, 1946, in Lake Hiawatha, New Jersey
Home: San Francisco, California

SELECTED TITLES

The Snail's Spell
1982

The Night Flight
1985

Step Into the Night
1988

Where Butterflies Grow
1989

Lizard in the Sun
1990

Under Your Feet
1990

Sea Elf
1993

My Father's Hands
1994

Bears Out There
1995

Earthdance
1996

Tyrannosaurus Time
1999

Each Living Thing
2000

As a child growing up in Lake Hiawatha, New Jersey, and Brooklyn, New York, Joanne loved playing outdoors. In Lake Hiawatha, where Joanne lived for her first five years, there were always animals to encounter. Joanne fondly recalls, "It was a wonderful place to explore, full of treasures to discover. There were just a few houses on our street, but there were woods all around, filled with small creatures."

Joanne's parents influenced her deeply. From her father, who was nicknamed "Bugs," Joanne learned to appreciate and try to understand nature. She warmly remembers, "My father liked to pick things up and examine them. He was the one who introduced me to nature up close. He would hold little creatures in his hand and say, 'Joanne, I have something really fabulous to show you.' Then he would open his fingers and show me whatever it was he had found—a beetle, a snail, a fuzzy caterpillar. Then he would let me hold it, and I could feel it move, wiggle, or crawl as I held it in my hand. So I became very comfortable holding tiny animals."

From her mother, who loved sunsets and hummingbirds, Joanne inherited a more poetic sense of nature. She says, "My mother would like to walk along the water and watch sunsets. She liked a much broader scope of nature, like the changing of the seasons. But the little, teeny, weeny, squiggly things with lots of legs—those were not her cup of tea! She belonged to the 'squish' school. Her theory was, if you see a bug, squish it!"

Science and Wonder

Part scientist, part poet, Joanne absorbed the lessons of her parents. She looks to nature for information and enjoyment. And often she finds something more: "Going for a walk instantly calms me down," Joanne says. "It gives me a peaceful feeling. My problems often seem insignificant when I observe the natural world and witness its cycles. There's so much to discover—whether it's a

flock of geese overhead or the fat, round moon rising in the sky once again."

"I've had a great many pets—including rabbits, salamanders, ducks, pigeons, canaries, hamsters, fish, and snails—and some of them have found their way into my books."

Joanne believes the natural world is even more wonderful when you begin to unlock its secrets. That is the job of the scientist. "Science is all around us," she firmly states. "We are science. Our bodies are science. We shouldn't be so afraid of that word, because so much of science is fascinating. It brings us closer to our world."

In many of Joanne's books about nature, she invites readers to let loose their imagination. Combining fantasy and factual insight, they are asked to become another creature—to creep on long padded toes like a lizard, to shake the snow from their fur like a great bear, to stuff acorns inside their furry cheeks like a chipmunk. The journey is always strange and exciting, filled with wonder and delight.

It's hard for many readers to understand the time that goes into writing a book. Joanne says,

"When you look at the artwork, you can see the time that's put into it. But you can't see the time that goes into writing the five hundred words in a picture book. You figure it probably took a very short amount of time. You don't realize that what you read is only the tip of the iceberg—and the rest of the iceberg is all the research and the many drafts that didn't make it."

Joanne loves her life as a writer. She tells this story: "When I see kids on school visits, I ask them, 'What do you think I do as a writer?' They say that I sit at a desk and write. I show them a photograph of me walking in Golden Gate Park and say, 'This is me hard at work!' A writer can be working even when he or she is outside looking at a tree. There are so many things around you that can trigger your imagination and fill your mind with images and words."

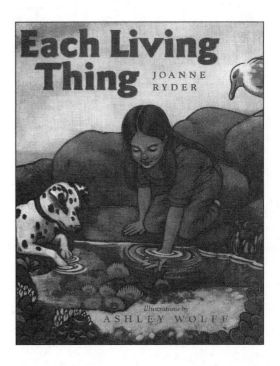

DO IT YOURSELF!

Joanne Ryder says, "I just got a batch of stories from kids who modeled their stories after my Just-for-a-Day books (*Winter Whale, Sea Elf, Lizard in the Sun,* and more). They became endangered animals for a day. They were really neat stories." Give it a try! Remember, like Joanne, you'll have to choose an endangered animal, learn facts about it, and try to imagine what it feels like to be that animal. Have fun!

Cynthia Rylant

Born: June 6, 1954, in Hopewell, Virginia
Home: Pacific Northwest

SELECTED TITLES

When I Was Young in the Mountains
(Caldecott Honor Book)
1982

The Relatives Came
(Caldecott Honor Book)
1985

A Fine White Dust
(Newbery Honor Book)
1986

Henry and Mudge
(first in a series)
1987

All I See
1988

Appalachia: The Voices of Sleeping Birds
1991

Missing May
(Newbery Medal)
1992

Mr. Putter and Tabby Pour the Tea
(first in a series)
1994

Poppleton
(first in a series)
1997

Cat Heaven
1997

Scarecrow
1998

"I grew up in rural West Virginia," says Cynthia Rylant, "and what happened there deeply affects what I write."

She recalls a simple, unadorned life—a life without indoor plumbing until she was eight years old, without much money, without picture books, without a local bookstore or even a local library. In fact, Cynthia never saw the inside of a library until she went away to college.

"Literature and the arts weren't really a part of my growing up," Cynthia admits. "Growing up in a rural area in a coal-mining family, you really can't see much more for yourself than what's in front of you."

Withdrawn and sensitive, Cynthia also experienced her share of pain and loss. Her parents separated when she was only four. She never really got to know her father, who died at an early age. "I did not have a chance to know him or to say good-bye to him," Cynthia laments, "and that is all the loss I needed to become a writer."

Still, Cynthia describes her childhood world as "a small sparkling universe that gave me a lifetime's worth of material for my writing." She adds, "I think it

was the isolation and insulation of my early years that made me turn inward and just mostly concentrate on what people say, and the things they do in their kitchens and living rooms."

Later Cynthia would think of these small, domestic moments as "life's profound experiences." These are the simple things that recur again and again in her writing: family and friends, beloved pets, deep feelings, and hard-earned wisdom, all fueled by cherished memories of growing up in Appalachia.

Cynthia attended college with the notion of becoming a nurse. But once there, she was introduced to great literature and became a voracious reader. Slowly, inside her, an idea formed. Cynthia dreamed of becoming a writer.

After college Cynthia found a job in the local library. To her great delight, she was assigned to the children's room. And she fell in love—with children's books! "I

can't tell you how I loved that room and all those books I never knew existed," Cynthia enthuses. "I carried bags full home at night just to read for pleasure."

Fearful of failure, Cynthia quietly set out to write a book of her own. It was to be a reflective book, drawing upon her Appalachian upbringing. She remembers, "One night I sat down and wrote *When I Was Young in the Mountains*. I sent it to a New York publisher. And it sold."

Her life would never be the same.

While many authors are strictly disciplined, forcing themselves to write a few hours each day, Cynthia is not. She admits, "Most times, I write picture books in about an hour. And that's it. I just sit down and write one and I'm done." Equally surprising, Cynthia rarely revises her work.

Relying on inspiration, memory, and her love of language, Cynthia writes in creative bursts. "As I do the writing," she explains, "I'm just lost for a couple of hours and then I come back and I see what I've put on paper." She confesses, "I could never be one of those writers who does it simply for pleasure and keeps a little journal tucked inside a dresser drawer. *Never.* That doesn't mean I don't love my work. But I view it as exactly that: *It is work*, and there has to be more reward than just me reading it and putting it in the drawer."

Of course, for Cynthia, there is reward—plenty. She has excelled in every form she's attempted, and Cynthia has tried nearly all of them: young adult novels, easy-to-read chapter books, picture books, biography, and poetry! Her work is widely praised and has garnered critical awards, including the coveted Newbery Medal. But for Cynthia, writing itself has provided a far greater reward: "Writing has given me a sense of self-worth that I didn't have my whole childhood. I am really proud of that. The books have carried me through some troubled times and have made me feel that I am worthy of having a place on this earth."

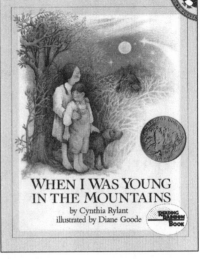

WHEN I WAS YOUNG IN THE MOUNTAINS
by Cynthia Rylant
illustrated by Diane Goode

DO IT YOURSELF!

Animals appear often in Cynthia's books. It only makes sense, since Cynthia admits, "All of my life has been filled with pets. They are on my desk, under my table, in my lap, beside the door." Do you have any pets? If so, think about using your pet as a character in a story! If not, imagine a pet you would like to have, and write a story about it.

Allen Say

Born: August 28, 1937, in Yokohama, Japan
Home: San Francisco, California

SELECTED TITLES

The Bicycle Man
1982

How My Parents Learned to Eat
1984

The Boy of the Three-Year Nap
(Caldecott Honor Book)
1988

A River Dream
1988

The Lost Lake
1989

El Chino
1990

Tree of Cranes
1991

Grandfather's Journey
(Caldecott Medal)
1993

Allison
1997

Tea With Milk
1999

The Sign Painter
2000

Growing up in Japan during World War II would have been hard for any child. For Allen Say, a shy, unathletic child, it was especially difficult. "I was a very sickly child," says Allen, perhaps with a slight trace of sadness at the memory. "My mother tells me that I suffered from every childhood disease known to medicine. I was a weakling, really."

Because of the war, Allen's family was forced to move often. "I was terrified of new schools and teachers," Allen admits. "That's what happens when you go to seven different grade schools. I was made to fight bullies at every school. So I escaped into reading and drawing. The marvelous thing that happened to me was that during recess I would draw. Students would stand behind me and watch. That's probably the first time I discovered that I had this power— it was the only power I had."

Though Allen was obviously a talented artist, his father had different ambitions for his son. He wanted Allen to become a businessman. Allen recalls, "My parents were horrified. This was a disaster, to have their number one son turning into an artist. They tried everything to discourage me. I rebelled, of course; I drew."

After the war, normal life slowly returned to Japan. For the first time in years, Allen's family settled down in one place. But a new difficulty soon arose: His parents divorced. "It was a very traumatic experience for me," Allen confides.

Allen was sent to live with his father's mother, a strict disciplinarian. "We didn't like each other," Allen admits. "She didn't want to have me there and I didn't want to be there." Soon a deal was reached: Allen's grandmother gave him the money to find another place to live. Each month she handed him an envelope filled with money, with which he would pay his rent and buy his food and anything else he needed. By age 12, Allen Say had his own apartment.

Suddenly life took a dramatic turn for the better. Allen fulfilled a dream—he was hired as a

cartoonist's apprentice. He recalls, "I had always wanted to become a cartoonist, so I went out and looked for my favorite, Noro Shinpei, one of the most famous cartoonists in Japan. I begged him to take me on as his student."

> *"The father I talked about in The Lost Lake was me. It was probably my way of saying I'm sorry to my own daughter because I wasn't spending enough time with her."*

Working after school and on weekends, Allen drew for hours every day, improving his craft by helping with the great master's comic strips. He found time for his schoolwork late at night. After all, Allen could stay up as late as he liked—there was no one around to tell him when to go to bed.

Moving to California

Allen's father resettled in California and sent for Allen to come live with him. It was a challenge to face a new country and its new ways. He says, "I didn't speak any English at all. I said to myself, 'Where am I? What is this?'"

Allen gradually grew to enjoy life in the States. At the same time, a new interest emerged: photography. After he finished school, Allen gave up his dream of becoming an artist and began a career as a photographer. Still, he dabbled from time to time with watercolors and pen and ink.

"My first book was done in my photo studio," Allen recalls. "I began to draw and a story came out. It was called *Dr. Smith's Safari*." But even with this success—and the success of later books—Allen didn't take children's books seriously. For him it was only a hobby, something he did between photo assignments.

One day Allen reluctantly accepted a job illustrating a manuscript called *The Boy of the Three-Year Nap*. He decided to do one last children's book and then call it quits. "But a strange thing happened," Allen remembers. "I started painting the pictures and I went back to my boyhood—into my master's studio—and all the memories came back to me. I remembered all the joys of painting." That was the turning point. Allen Say had finally, at long last, found his joy. From that moment forward, Allen dedicated himself to writing and illustrating children's books.

Grandfather's Journey

ALLEN SAY

DO IT YOURSELF!

Allen Say tells us: "All good artists have an excellent memory. You have to remember. You cannot imagine without memory. The great writer James Joyce said, 'The imagination is memory.' So that's my advice: Remember." Write a short story or draw a picture based upon one of your childhood memories. If, like Allen, you'd like to change a detail or two, go right ahead. That's part of the fun!

Jon Scieszka

Born: September 8, 1954, in Flint, Michigan
Home: Brooklyn, New York

SELECTED TITLES

The True Story of the 3 Little Pigs!
1989

The Frog Prince, Continued
1991

Knights of the Kitchen Table
(first in the Time Warp Trio series)
1991

The Stinky Cheese Man and Other Fairly Stupid Tales
(Caldecott Honor Book)
1992

The Book That Jack Wrote
1994

Math Curse
1995

Squids Will Be Squids: Fresh Morals, Beastly Fables
1998

Baloney, Henry P.
2001

If there were a training ground for children's writers, then Jon Scieszka (rhymes with *Fresca*) went to it: He was a school teacher for ten years, teaching first through eighth grades. As a teacher, Jon got to see what made kids tick—the things they liked and didn't like, what made them worry and wonder, what made children upset and what caused them to laugh out loud.

Jon took note of it all—especially what made kids laugh. A natural comic, Jon delights in silly, goofy humor and has a lifelong affection for absurdity. After all, as Jon readily admits, "I was the kid in the back of the class, cracking jokes, thinking up weird stuff, goofing around."

Jon claims, "All of my writing comes out of having been a teacher and having learned from kids. I was in teaching long enough to come around to what all good teachers always realize: That they're actually learning more than they're teaching or giving out. The more you shut up and allow kids to learn, the better off you are. I'm thrilled to have that in my bones now."

Equally important, Jon respects kids. He believes that children are smarter than most people give them credit for—capable of appreciating sophisticated stories and twisted humor. Says Jon, "My working motto and guiding principle in writing is Never Underestimate the Intelligence of Your Audience."

After college, Jon gained a master's degree in writing from Columbia University. But success as a writer did not come instantly. For years Jon dreamed of writing "the great American novel." One thing he did not dream about, however, was writing for children. While Jon labored over his writing— penning short stories for adults— he worked a variety of jobs to help make ends meet. After painting New York City apartments for five years, Jon became a teacher.

Over time, thanks in large part to his daily contact with school-age children, Jon decided to try his hand at writing children's books. He explains, "I came up with the

idea for *The True Story of the Three Little Pigs!* after rewriting fairy tales with my second-grade class."

> **"I think that turning something upside down or doing something wrong is the peak of what's funny to second-graders."**

Soon even Fate had to crack a smile: Jon met illustrator Lane Smith, and an instant friendship—and an award-winning partnership—was formed. Jon showed Lane the manuscript and Lane—a quirky, gifted artist—loved the story's freshness, originality, and skewed humor.

Jon recalls, "I knew Lane would do a great job because we like a lot of the same cartoons and books and ideas. And we laugh at each other's bad jokes all the time. Our audience is hardcore, silly kids, and there are a lot of 'em out there!"

But a not-so-funny thing happened on the road to best-selling success: Nearly every publisher rejected the story! "People thought the manuscript was too weird, too sophisticated," Jon explains. "People don't give kids enough credit. When I taught second-graders, that's the age when they first discover parody. They're just getting those reading skills, and nothing cracks them up like a joke that turns stuff upside down."

Today, *The True Story of the Three Little Pigs!* is considered a classic. A landmark in boisterous buffoonery, it's been translated into ten languages. This makes Jon partly responsible, in other words, for spreading goofiness around the globe. More important, his picture books—and his popular Time Warp Trio series—have answered a need for fun, action-packed books that children, in particular, boys, will eagerly read and enjoy.

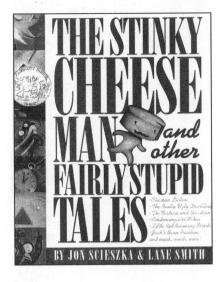

These days Jon is developing a literacy campaign aimed at boys, the so-called reluctant readers. As a teacher, Jon worked with "hard to reach" boys on a daily basis. "These guys are just like me and my brothers," Jon says. "They want action; they want something goofy; they don't want to sit down."

When it comes to getting ideas, Jon explains, "You have to give ideas room to grow. And give yourself the time and energy to purely think about things and goof around with them. I'm a big fan of fiddling around with ideas and seeing what takes hold."

DO IT YOURSELF!

Jon Scieszka has produced some wonderful stories by taking traditional folktales and turning them upside down. Usually he begins by telling the story from a new, surprising perspective (the wolf in *True Story*; the frog in *The Frog Prince, Continued*). Try it yourself. Begin with any familiar folktale—for example, "Goldilocks and the Three Bears," "The Emperor's New Clothes," or "The Three Billy Goats Gruff." Then try telling it from a different point of view. Ask yourself how that poor, misunderstood troll under the bridge would tell *his* version of "The Three Billy Goats Gruff"?

Maurice Sendak

Born: June 10, 1928, in Brooklyn, New York
Home: Ridgefield, Connecticut

SELECTED TITLES

Little Bear
(first in a series)
1957

The Nutshell Library
1962

Where the Wild Things Are
(Caldecott Medal)
1963

Hector Protector
1965

Higglety Pigglety Pop!
1967

In the Night Kitchen
(Caldecott Honor Book)
1970

Outside Over There
(Caldecott Honor Book)
1981

The Nutcracker
1984

Dear Mili
1988

I Saw Esau
1992

The Miami Giant
1995

Swine Lake
1999

Maurice Sendak believes that children live in two worlds—fantasy and reality. *Where the Wild Things Are*, his acclaimed masterpiece, reflects that belief. Max, the hero of the book, moves from reality to fantasy and back to reality again. Sendak comments, "Through fantasy, Max discharges his anger against his mother and returns to the real world sleepy, hungry, and at peace with himself."

Sendak believes that it's important for children to have a lively imagination. And for an artist it is essential. "Fantasy is the core of all writing for children, as I think it is for the writing of any book, for any creative act, perhaps for the act of living," he says. "But these fantasies have to be given physical form, so you build a house around them. And the house is what you call a story. And the painting of the house is the bookmaking. But essentially it's a dream or a fantasy."

Make no mistake: Sendak's fantasy stories are about real life. His books often deal with everyday feelings such as anger and fear. Some critics believe the books are too frightening for young children. Sendak disagrees:

"Children know a lot more than people give them credit for. Children are willing to deal with many dubious subjects that grown-ups think they shouldn't know about. But children are small, courageous people who have to deal every day with a multitude of problems, just as we adults do."

The Influence of Early Days

Perhaps more than any artist, Maurice Sendak draws his inspiration from memories of his early childhood. For example, *In the Night Kitchen* was inspired by an advertisement Sendak remembered from childhood. He recalls, "The advertisement was for the Sunshine Bakers. And the advertisement read, 'We Bake While You Sleep!'"

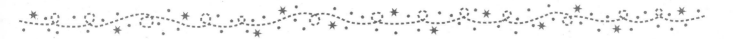

Strangely, the advertisement upset and angered young Maurice. He wanted to stay up all night to see what the grown-ups did! "I remember I used to save the coupons showing the three fat little Sunshine Bakers going off to this yummy place, wherever it was, to have their fun, while I had to go to bed. The book was a way to get back at them and say that now I'm old enough to stay up late and see what's going on in the night kitchen."

"Writing is very difficult and gives me a great deal of pleasure, partly because it is so difficult."

Sendak drew upon a childhood fear for his favorite book, *Outside Over There.* "Much of it is based on what scared me when I was little. I remember as a very small child seeing a book about a little girl who is caught in a rainstorm. She's wearing a huge yellow slicker and boots. The rain comes down harder and harder and begins to rise and spill into her boots, and that's when I would always stop looking at the book. It scared me too much. I never found out what happened to the little girl."

A sickly boy, Maurice did not have a happy childhood. He remembers, "I was miserable as a kid—I couldn't make friends, I couldn't play stoopball, I couldn't skate. I stayed home and drew pictures. When I wanted to go out and do something, my father would say, 'You'll catch a cold.' And I did. I did whatever he told me."

Isolated by illness as a child, Maurice withdrew into a life of fantasy. And he fed his fantasy life with books. He says, "I felt that books were holy objects, to be caressed, rapturously sniffed, and devotedly provided for. I gave my life to them. I still do. I continue to do what I did as a child—dream of books, make books, and collect books."

Today Maurice Sendak values the fact that his readers are children. What he likes most about children is their honesty. "I long ago discovered that they are the best audience. They certainly make the best critics," Sendak said. "When children love your book, it's 'I love your book, thank you, I want to marry you when I grow up.' Or it's 'Dear Mr. Sendak: I hate your book. Hope you die soon. Cordially.'"

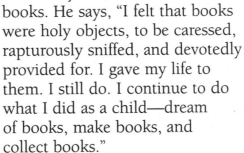

DO IT YOURSELF!

Dreams are like messages from the imagination. Leave paper and a pen beside your bed. When you wake in the morning, try to remember your dreams. Before getting up, spend a few minutes writing them down. Who knows? Someday these dreams might inspire a fantastic story.

Dr. Seuss (Theodor Seuss Geisel)

Born: March 2, 1904, in Springfield, Massachusetts
Died: September 24, 1991

SELECTED TITLES

Where did Dr. Seuss get all of his wonderfully wacky ideas? "I get all my ideas in Switzerland near the Forka Pass," Dr. Seuss once explained, tongue planted firmly in cheek. "There is a little town called Gletch, and two thousand feet up above Gletch there is a smaller hamlet called Ober Gletch. I go there on the fourth of August every summer to get my cuckoo clock repaired. While the cuckoo is in the hospital, I wander around and talk to the people in the streets. They are very strange people, and I get my ideas from them."

Of course, Seuss wasn't serious. But he was seriously poking fun at the notion that authors can ever really know where their ideas come from. That's the way the mind of Dr. Seuss worked: He often used nonsense to make a point.

"Nonsense wakes up the brain cells."

"Anything can spark an idea," Seuss claimed. And believe it or not, once an idea blew in through an open window. Seuss was at his drawing table, aimlessly doodling. Suddenly a gentle breeze blew a drawing he had made of an elephant on top of another drawing he had made of a tree. Seuss remembered, "I said to myself, an elephant in a tree! What's he doing there? Finally I said to myself, 'Of course! He's hatching an egg!'" Seuss had discovered the idea for his next book, *Horton Hatches the Egg*.

For Seuss, doodling was a favorite technique used to conjure up ideas. For example, he once drew a picture of a turtle sitting on top of another turtle. Seuss kept drawing until there was a huge pile of turtles stacked one on top of the other. He looked at the preposterous pile of turtles and asked himself, "Why? What does this mean?" (To discover how Seuss answered the question, you'll have to read *Yertle the Turtle and Other Stories*!)

Pure Nonsense...
Or Is It?

You should know that Dr. Seuss wasn't the author's birth name; it's a pseudonym invented by the writer. His real name was Theodor Seuss Geisel (pronounced "GUY-zel"). There isn't a more famous children's author in the world. His books are witty, weird, wacky, wild, and wonderful. But most of all, they are read and read and read again. Today there are more than 200 million copies of Dr. Seuss's books in print. And those books have been translated into 17 languages.

Seuss has invented some of the strangest, most memorable characters in all of literature. There's Horton, Bartholomew Cubbins, the Zooks and the Sneetches, the Grinch, the Cat in the Hat, the Tufted Gustard, and the lovable Lorax! How did he come up with all of those weird names? "That's the easy part," Seuss claimed. "I can look at an animal and know what it is."

Seuss's interest in animals blossomed when he was just a little boy and his father ran a zoo in Massachusetts. Seuss would visit with a sketchpad, stand outside the cages, and draw all the animals. Of course, he drew them his own way! Seuss admitted, "I can't draw real animals. I'm a cartoonist, not an artist."

Dr. Seuss often used silly characters and strange lands as metaphors—a crafty, sideways approach to real-life's more serious issues. His books have addressed important topics such as nuclear weapons (*The Butter Battle Book*), protecting the environment (*The Lorax*), and racial prejudice (*The Sneetches and Other Stories*).

The revered author saw little difference between kids and adults. He once said, "I feel the same about kids as I do about adults— some are delightful, some are dreadful. Most writers of kids' books will tell you all children are wonderful, but they're not."

Though his wife, Audrey, had two children from a previous marriage, Dr. Seuss never had any children of his own. Why no kids for the famous children's book author? Seuss said, thinking of his many readers, "I have 200 million kids. That's enough."

Theodor Seuss Geisel passed away in 1991, at the age of 87. His "200 million kids," many of whom are now adults with kids of their own, remain devoted fans of the colorful, wacky, and playful world that Dr. Seuss created in his books.

DO IT YOURSELF!

Dr. Seuss often got ideas by doodling. He'd draw a picture and then ask himself, "Why? How did this happen?" Then he invented a story to explain it. You can try this technique, too. If you don't like to draw, you can always look at pictures in magazines. Find an interesting picture that strikes your fancy. Then make up a story about it—let your imagination run wild!

Marjorie Weinman Sharmat

Born: November 12, 1928, in Portland, Maine
Home: Tucson, Arizon

SELECTED TITLES

Getting Something on Maggie Marmelstein
(first in a series)
1971

Nate the Great
(first in a series)
1972

Mooch the Messy
1976

I'm Terrific
1977

A Big, Fat Enormous Lie
1978

Mitchell Is Moving
1978

The 329th Friend
1979

Gila Monsters Meet You at the Airport
1980

Tiffany Dino Works Out
1995

Hollywood Hound
(first in a series)
2000

"My earliest ambition," confides author Marjorie Weinman Sharmat, "was to become a writer or a detective or a lion tamer.

"I began writing when I was eight. A friend and I published a newspaper called *The Snooper's Gazette* that we filled with news we obtained by spying on grown-ups for our detective agency. It achieved a circulation of about four—her parents and mine."

Marjorie's lifelong fascination with detective work led her to create one of the most beloved characters in contemporary children's literature: the pint-sized private eye, Nate the Great, who is ably assisted by his loyal mutt, Sludge.

For Marjorie, it was love at first write: "I loved Nate from the very beginning," she says. Inspired, in part, by the deadpan dialogue of the *Dragnet* television series, Nate is a tough-talking sleuth with a nose for intrigue and a stomach for pancakes. Thanks to his dogged determination and unconventional brand of logic, Nate is still solving mysteries— nearly 30 years after his first case.

It's a challenge for Marjorie to keep coming up with ideas for new mysteries. She explains,

"Increasingly, I've found that I've been working backward on my Nate cases. I look for something unusual but plausible for the ending, and then I create a case leading up to it. Fortunately, the characterizations and dialogue always fall into place easily, and the twists and turns of plot arise from knowing where I'm going and trying to keep readers from finding out too soon."

Marjorie has had plenty of help over the years from her family. First and foremost, there's her husband, Mitchell Sharmat. While other authors must contend with the turmoil of writer's block, Marjorie has her own unique solution close at hand—she simply hollers, "Help!"

"If I run into a problem," Marjorie says, "I just ask my husband. In fact, my husband came up with

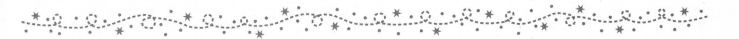

the solution to the first Nate book. He helped me with so many books over the years, I finally encouraged him to write his own." Marjorie adds: "One of Mitch's titles, *Gregory, the Terrible Eater*, is the most successful book to come out of this household. I take great joy in his success."

> **"I like to write funny books because I think that life is basically a serious business and needs a humorous counterbalance."**

Marjorie also credits her two sons, Craig and Andrew, for inspiring many episodes in her books. Craig, who is a musician, cowrote *Nate the Great and the Musical Note*. Marjorie's sister Rosalind suggested the premise and title for *Nate the Great and the Pillowcase* and eventually became its coauthor. The concept for *Gila Monsters Meet You at the Airport* stemmed directly from an experience Andrew had when the Sharmat family decided to move from New York to Arizona. Marjorie remembers, "Before leaving, Andrew was warned by his friends about the strange things he would find out West, and when he arrived here, he discovered that his new western friends had rather wild ideas of what the East was like. Out of all this came *Gila Monsters Meet You at the Airport*."

Shy and Introspective

Marjorie grew up in Portland, Maine. "I was introspective, nearsighted, and shy," she says, "and I still am. I was the stereotype: the glasses, staying indoors, and really loving books. I had friends, but there was a part of me that was reserved from the outside world. I just seemed to communicate better with characters in books."

Reading Marjorie's books, it becomes clear that she brings a unique sensitivity to her work. She writes with compassion and understanding, and always roots for the underdog. "Loneliness is a theme that, perhaps above all others, appeals to me as a writer," Marjorie reveals. "I feel for people who are not one of the gang."

Most of Marjorie's writing begins with an idea for a character. Whether shy like Vanessa, egocentric like Jason Everett Bear, or simply irrepressible like Maggie Marmelstein, they all seem to share one trait: "They boss me around," Marjorie complains with a laugh. "They tell me what they want to do. And I sort of feverishly try to keep up with them!"

DO IT YOURSELF!

Write your own mystery involving a detective. But first, listen to Marjorie's advice: "A lot of my Nate books are based on things that have happened to me. If something interesting occurs, I'll always ask myself, 'Could this happen to Nate?'" Marjorie adds one more tip: "A mystery needs a satisfying solution, so try to think of a solution before you start the story."

Peter Sis

Born: May 11, 1949, in Brno, Moravia, Czechoslovakia
Home: New York, New York

Growing up in Czechoslovakia, Peter Sis often found himself daydreaming about distant lands and the adventures of explorers. In the 1950s and 1960s, Czechoslovakia was a land ruled by the iron fist of the Soviet government. Citizens had limited political and cultural freedoms. Travel beyond "the Iron Curtain"—the invisible border that separated the Western world from the Communist world—was not allowed for most citizens.

Peter explains: "People can't choose if they live in a time of war or peace. It's amazing, though, that even within that very undesirable world we had time to play our games and have fun as children always do. In retrospect, I think I had a wonderful childhood, mostly thanks to my parents."

Because of his special status as a filmmaker, Peter's father was given the rare opportunity to travel beyond the country's borders. Peter recalls how his father's stories opened Peter's imagination to the world beyond his day-to-day experiences. "I would sit in the kitchen," Peter relates, "and he would describe things that I would never otherwise have been able to comprehend."

Though his parents warned him that an artist's life can be lonely and demanding, Peter felt certain that it was for him. Formal art school, however, provided a rude awakening. Then in his early teens, he soon became frustrated with the school's restrictions. He explains, "The teachers wanted us to draw absolutely according to the style of the nineteenth century. It was very hard because there was really no space for fantasy or individuality."

Yet Peter persevered and graduated with a solid foundation of technical skill to complement his rich imagination. And he also found a new love: film animation. His work as an animator and short-filmmaker opened new doors for Peter. "The Czech government let me out to work on a Swiss television series, but the situation was getting more

and more difficult," he explains. "All the money I earned would go to the film company or the government of Prague, and I would only get a small percentage of it. Most of all, I was never sure each time I returned home that they would ever let me out again."

- - - - - - - - - - - - - - - - - - -

"The most enjoyable part of creating a book is doing the initial sketches, putting the book together, the thinking part."

- - - - - - - - - - - - - - - - - - -

Peter began to feel increasingly trapped in his own country. In 1982 he was allowed to travel to Los Angeles, California, to work on a film project linked with the 1984 Summer Olympic Games. Once again politics intervened. The Soviet Union and its satellite nations suddenly pulled out of the Olympics. Peter remembers it well: "The Czech passport office said that I should return home. But I had just had enough. I simply didn't go back."

Following the Dream

It was a trying time for the struggling artist in a strange, new world. "I just couldn't figure out how things worked. I was in Los Angeles showing my work to people from the galleries who commission art, and they kept saying 'It's too European, it's too dark.' I was confused by it all."

At a friend's suggestion, Peter sent a sample of his work to the children's author Maurice Sendak. Impressed with Peter's work, Maurice called Peter and eventually introduced him to Ava Weiss, the art director of Greenwillow Books. She offered Peter a job immediately. His life as a children's book illustrator had begun.

Peter moved to New York City, the center of publishing in the United States. Under the spell of new sights and impressions, he absorbed the vibrant life of New York's streets and people. Peter sold illustrations to magazines such as *The New York Times Book Review* and *The Atlantic Monthly*. And he created children's books— remarkable books full of magic and wonder.

One of Peter's most personal books is *Follow the Dream*, his artistic interpretation of Columbus's discovery of the New World. A book of stunning beauty and insight, *Follow the Dream* was inspired by Peter's own discovery of a new world. Peter wrote: "Columbus didn't let the walls hold him back. For him, the outside world was not to be feared but explored. And so he followed his dream."

DO IT YOURSELF!

Peter's parents used to give him assignments. They would suggest a concept, and, after a few weeks of thinking about it, Peter would have to produce an illustration based on that idea. Try it yourself with this assignment: Think about Peter's life—about walls, freedom, and being a poor artist from Europe suddenly finding yourself in Los Angeles or New York. Now draw a picture—it can be any picture you want—based on those impressions. Remember, as Peter says, "Anything goes!"

Lane Smith

Born: August 25, 1959, in Tulsa, Oklahoma
Home: New York, New York

SELECTED TITLES

Although Lane Smith had already published two children's books, it wasn't until *The True Story of the Three Little Pigs!* that people really began to take him seriously. Well, not exactly seriously, but at least people did start to *notice* him. That's when most readers began to realize that Lane Smith was, well, different.

Lane remembers touring schools with Jon Scieszka. It was a new experience for Lane. He recalls, "My problem was that I would get in there and the kids would start throwing stuff around and acting stupid. I didn't know how else to get them to be quiet, so I'd throw something at them and be just as goofy. It's hard for me to be a serious authority figure. Someone will yell out, 'Hey, can you draw Bart Simpson with a hatchet in his head?' and I'll say, 'Okay! Got any red markers?'"

The visits were riotous events. Jon would read some of his stories, and Lane would draw along as he read. "I felt like Zippy the Drawing Chimp," Lane recalls with a laugh. "Jon would be reading and I'd be frantically trying to catch up with my drawings. I felt like I should be wearing a clown suit, making balloon animals. But actually, it's helpful to visit classrooms and see what kids respond to. You say the word *stinky* and they're rolling on the floor." That observation, by the way, led to another of Jon and Lane's collaborations, *The Stinky Cheese Man and Other Fairly Stupid Tales.*

A Nice, Quiet Kid

For the first three years of his life, Lane lived in Tulsa, Oklahoma. Then his family moved to Corona, California. "I was always drawing," Lane recounts. "And I was always writing little stories and odd things. I wasn't very social. I think that's why I decided on art as a career—it's such a nice, solitary thing to do. You can be by yourself and sit in a room and come up with all these goofy ideas."

Each summer Lane and his family would drive back to Oklahoma to visit relatives and friends. That's

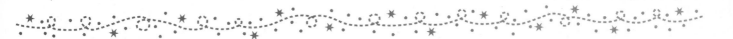

when Lane's love of popular culture began. "We'd take the old Route 66," Lane fondly recalls. "We'd see the classic, kitschy America—Stucky gas stations, giant doughnut stands, concrete tepee motels—and I think that was a great influence on my work."

> **"There are so many serious books out there and lots of people who do them really well. But there aren't many people who do really goofy work. It's so refreshing to see kids respond to funny stuff."**

These are some of the other things that influence Lane's art: old *Monty Python* television shows, comic books, Disneyland, Las Vegas, ugly shirts, *Mad* magazine, tacky wallpaper, European illustration, and anything else that makes his eyes light up. "My style is just a combination of everything I've put into my brain over the years—Paul Klee and Buster Keaton and Tex Avery. All this stuff mixes up and hopefully comes out in my own style."

Today Lane works in a Manhattan studio not far from his home. He is a determined, if somewhat sporadic, worker. "I like to take breaks," he admits. "I might take a break to watch cartoons, but it

will sort of inspire me. Or I might sit down—I usually surround myself with all sorts of kids' books and stuff—and just read some James Marshall for half an hour. When I go back to my work, I can see it fresh again."

In 1992 Lane Smith won a Caldecott Honor for *The Stinky Cheese Man.* Lane says, "It is the book that I am the most pleased with from beginning to end. The stories work on their own; it works as a whole; and its transitional elements give it a filmlike quality. It has running gags. It's completely resolved at the end. And," he says, saving the best for last, "it's really fun."

Winning such a prestigious award came as quite a surprise to Lane. "Traditionally, humor books haven't been taken very seriously. And even though people seem to like the book," Lane confesses, "it is kind of gross in parts. The stories are zany and the humor is sort of over the top; we have eyeballs bugging out and all that. So it was a total shock when teachers and librarians said they liked it. I was really honored."

DO IT YOURSELF!

Lane Smith and Jon Scieszka work together on many projects. Lane describes the process: "Jon will write something, and I'll draw something to accompany it. He'll crack up and add a line of type, and then I'll complement that with some other sketch. We play off each other really well." Try it yourself. Team up with a friend and try writing a story together—two heads just might be better than one!

131

Peter Spier

Born: June 6, 1927, in Amsterdam, Netherlands
Home: Shoreham, New York

SELECTED TITLES

The Fox Went Out on a Chilly Night
(Caldecott Honor Book)
1961

London Bridge Is Falling Down!
1967

The Erie Canal
1970

The Star-Spangled Banner
1973

Tin-Lizzie
1975

Noah's Ark
(Caldecott Medal)
1977

Bored—Nothing to Do!
1978

The Legend of New Amsterdam
1979

People
1980

Peter Spier's Rain
1982

Father, May I Come?
1993

One fine afternoon in New England, Peter Spier and his wife, Kay, drove through the rolling landscape of the Berkshire Mountains admiring the leaves, which had turned a beautiful array of crimson reds, sun yellows, and burnished golds. Their hearts were light, and together they sang a favorite old folksong: *The fox went out on a chilly night, and he prayed to the moon to give him light, for he'd many miles to go that night before he reached the town-o, town-o, town-o.*

Suddenly struck with a new idea, Peter turned to Kay and asked, "Hey, wouldn't this area be a great setting for a picture book about that song?" Peter returned the next week, sketchbook in hand. He sketched old houses, barns, chicken coops, covered bridges, and more. From these observations, Peter created his award-winning book *The Fox Went Out on a Chilly Night.*

Peter often takes to the road when he is creating a book. "If I have to draw someplace and I don't know what it looks like," he says, "I'll go there with a sketchbook in my hand. If it's a city, for example, I'll check into a hotel and roam the streets for the next week. I'll sketch, observe, and make notes." Peter adds with conviction, "That's how you learn to draw."

Growing Up in Holland

Peter grew up in a small Dutch village named Broek-in-Waterland. But to get to school, he had to travel into the city of Amsterdam. Peter recalls the trip: "My brother, sister, and I would walk from our house to the tram, and during the winter, skate. The tram was an ancient swaying vehicle filled with the smoke of cigars and clay pipes, and with fishermen from the village of Volendam who wore huge wooden shoes and baggy pants. They were taking their catch to market. Herring and smoked eel were stacked in baskets in the aisles—an unforgettable aroma! After the tram ride, we took a ferry across the river. How I loved to be on the water in the early morning!

Then back on another tram and a short walk to our school."

- -

"When I wrote People, I was thinking that instead of holding our differences against each other, wouldn't it be better to rejoice in them."

- -

Peter's father, Joseph E.A. Spier, was a famous political cartoonist and journalist. Peter says that he owes a great deal of his drawing style to his father. "He was a great illustrator," Peter warmly recalls. "If you looked at his pictures next to mine, you'd see a great similarity—except that he drew much better than I do."

At the age of 25, after college and a three-year stint in the Royal Dutch Navy, Peter was offered work in the United States at a Dutch publishing company. He took the job, came to America, and has lived here ever since.

Acclaimed for his detailed panoramas and historical accuracy, Peter is one of the most respected artists in children's literature. His pictures are always full of activity, vitality, and humor. But equally important, Peter's books are expertly designed. Just as the words in a poem can create a pleasing rhythm, the variety in Peter's illustrations provides a welcome ebb and flow.

In *Peter Spier's Rain*, Spier balances many small pictures with dramatic, two-page spreads. Peter feels that these spreads provide places for the reader to rest, offering a space for thinking. He cites a different example from his Caldecott Medal winner, *Noah's Ark*: "On one spread you'll see a small picture of Noah picking the eggs and other pictures of the little things he must have done. But these details don't justify a full-page picture. They aren't important enough. Or look at the picture of the elephant standing on the mouse's tail—I do it to change the pace, to break the somberness, to give the book rhythm and something humorous."

At an age when most people have retired from their jobs, Peter Spier still has book projects in mind. "As long as your hand is steady, you can keep on making books for as long as you wish," he says happily. "The wonderful thing for me, at this stage of my life, is that I don't have to do it anymore. I'm doing it because it's still fun."

DO IT YOURSELF!

How did Peter Spier learn to draw so well? He gives one word: "Practice!" He also stresses the importance of drawing from real life. Peter, who often makes quick sketches of friends and neighbors, says, "Take a sketchbook outside and draw something. Once you capture a shape, it's yours forever. The same is true with writing. Stick to it, keep on doing it— and practice!"

133

William Steig

Born: November 14, 1907, in New York, New York
Home: Boston, Massachusetts

Writing and illustrating books isn't an overly complicated process for William Steig. He explains, "I begin by deciding it's time to write a book. And then I think about what animal I will use. It takes a while before things start happening. I can't truly say that I am ever inspired to write a book. It's the last thing in the world I think of until I have to do it. And then I count on my imagination to make things happen."

William Steig's imagination seems to be in good shape, because things certainly do happen in his books. In fact, pretty much anything can happen: a donkey finds a magic pebble (*Sylvester and the Magic Pebble*); a bone talks and casts magic spells (*The Amazing Bone*); and a boa constrictor falls in love with a garbage collector (*Tiffky Doofky*). Steig says, "I just ramble around and discover for myself what will happen next."

William Steig believes in working quickly. "I want to get it out of the way," he says. For him, too much thinking saddles the imagination. He once said, "It's only when you're consciously aware of what you're doing in a book that you're in trouble."

A Late Bloomer

William Steig grew up in a creative household, where artistic and musical pursuits were encouraged. As a child he loved to read; *Robinson Crusoe, Robin Hood,* and *Pinocchio* were his favorite books. *Robinson Crusoe*, in particular, seems to have had a lasting effect. In a way, *Abel's Island* is Steig's version of *Robinson Crusoe,* except in this case the stranded castaway is a mouse named Adelard Hassam di Chirico Flint!

Steig began his career as a cartoonist. The year was 1930, and the United States was in the throes of the Great Depression. To help support his family, Steig sold his first cartoon to *The New Yorker* magazine. It was the beginning of a long relationship; you can still find cartoons by William Steig in current issues of *The New Yorker.*

Steig found a job in advertising but, he says, "detested" it. Fortunately, in 1967, fellow *New Yorker* cartoonist and children's author Robert Kraus suggested that Steig try his hand at writing children's books. Steig jumped at the opportunity because he saw it as a way to leave advertising. His first book for children, *CDB!*, was soon published. And a new career had begun.

Although William Steig's illustrations have been widely praised, it is his way with words that readers seem to enjoy most. He uses all sorts of long, outrageous words, like *cantankerous* and *recumbent*, that are not usually found in picture books. He also uses made-up words, such as *dramberaberoomed* and *jibrakken sibibble digray*.

William Steig respects the intelligence of kids—that's why he doesn't hesitate to insert long words into his stories. But he's not sentimental and gushy about kids. Steig once said, "Every kid is a potential genius, but also a potential *yuckapuck*." (And although no one besides William Steig is quite sure what *yuckapuck* means, it probably isn't very nice.)

William Steig's career in children's books almost didn't happen. He never intended to become an author and illustrator. He once said, "If I'd had it my way, I'd have been a professional athlete, a sailor, a beachcomber, a painter, a gardener, a novelist, a banjo player, a traveler."

But for William Steig, life—like books—can't be planned in advance. Perhaps that's what he had in mind when he wrote *Dominic*. In the book, a dog sets out to see more of the world. Soon Dominic must choose between two paths: a road with "no surprise, nothing to discover or wonder at" or another road that promises to lead him to "where things will happen that you never could have guessed at—marvelous, unbelievable things." Like his creator, Dominic chose the second path: the one of surprise and adventure, the one where anything can happen. Even writing your first children's book at the age of 60!

DO IT YOURSELF!

When William Steig can't find the perfect word to describe a smell, sound, sight, or feeling, he makes one up. You won't find *dramberamberoomed* in any dictionary, but that doesn't mean there's a better way to describe a loud crash of thunder. Follow William Steig's example by making up words of your own. Be sure to write clear definitions for them. Use each of the new words in a sentence. Read the sentences to a friend. You'll have a *fantaburiffic* time!

John Steptoe

Born: September 14, 1950, in Brooklyn, New York
Died: August 28, 1989

In 1969, at age 19, John Lewis Steptoe came to national attention when his first book, *Stevie*, was hailed by *Life* magazine as "a new kind of book for black children."

Stevie was one of the first children's books to focus on black life in the ghetto. The colors of its illustrations were vibrant and alive; the words crackled with life and energy. In the book, Robert, an only child, must suddenly share his home with a smaller boy, Stevie. Listen to the words Steptoe used to describe Robert's first reaction to Stevie: *And so Stevie moved in with his old cry-baby self. He always had to have his way. And he was greedy too. Everything he sees he wants. 'Could I have somma that? Gimme this.' Man!*

In an interview with *The New York Times Book Review*, Steptoe commented, "I wrote the book for black children, therefore the language reflects it. I think black children need this. I wrote it this way because they are never spoken to. They always read about themselves as 'the Negro'—someone outside, not included."

John Steptoe did not have to look

far for story ideas. Almost all of his 16 books explore family and city life. And why not? John grew up in an apartment building in the Bedford-Stuyvesant section of Brooklyn, with his parents, two brothers, and a sister.

Growth and Change

"I love to change and grow," Steptoe said. And that is exactly what he did throughout his career. Although he illustrated his early books with lively, vibrant colors, Steptoe shifted to using only black ink, pencil, or charcoal. It was his way of challenging himself as an illustrator. The restricted use of color forced him to become a

better draftsperson. The culmination of this period came with his book *The Story of Jumping Mouse*.

The Story of Jumping Mouse is a Native American legend about a mouse who dreams of reaching a better, more beautiful world in "a far-off land." When John Steptoe first discovered the legend, he saw in the mouse character his own hopes and dreams for a better world. He said, "I heard this story several years ago, and it has always haunted me. It spoke to me about things that I would like to say to children."

"The more I read, the more reasons I found to be proud of my African ancestors."

John's greatest success came in 1987; after two-and-a-half years of work and research, he published *Mufaro's Beautiful Daughters*. It, too, was named a Caldecott Honor Book. And in it, all of John Steptoe's talents came together. Once again, he returned to the bright colors of his youth. But his illustrations were better somehow—richer, warmer, and more interesting. All of his years refining his craft had paid off.

Mufaro's Beautiful Daughters, dedicated to the children of South Africa, is based on an African folktale. In this fable, John found a new way to express his pride in his African heritage.

In his acceptance speech for the Caldecott award, Steptoe told the audience, "The award gives me hope that children who are still caught in the frustration of being black and poor in America will be encouraged to love themselves enough to accomplish the dreams I know are in their hearts."

On August 28, 1989, John Steptoe died of AIDS. He was 38 years old. Through John's books, many readers continue to be inspired by his hopes and dreams for a better world.

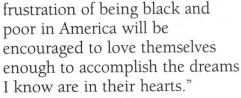

DO IT YOURSELF!

John Steptoe's book *Daddy Is a Monster... Sometimes* takes a playful look at why parents sometimes get very angry at their children. Write a funny story using a similar idea. Write about how when you misbehave, you can turn your parents into monsters. Or write about how a big or little sibling's annoying habits can turn you into a monster.

Mark Teague

Born: February 10, 1963, in San Diego, California
Home: Coxsackie, New York

SELECTED TITLES

The Trouble With the Johnsons
1989

Frog Medicine
1991

The Field Beyond the Outfield
1992

Pigsty
1994

The Iguana Brothers
1995

How I Spent My Summer Vacation
1995

The Secret Shortcut
1996

Poppleton (first in a series)
1997

The Lost and Found
1998

One Halloween Night
1999

How Do Dinosaurs Say Goodnight?
2000

Growing up, Mark Teague didn't necessarily think of himself as an artist or a writer. Sure, he drew a lot of pictures. And he wrote stories too. But to Mark it was natural, just another way of having fun—like playing soccer in the backyard or taking a walk through the woods.

Not much has changed. Mark still enjoys drawing pictures and making up stories. Only now he does it for a living. A self-taught artist, Mark doesn't think his work, at its heart, is all that different from what thousands and thousands of kids do quite naturally. "Artwork is free expression," Mark says. "With drawing, you should continue to feel free to do anything, and yet somehow as people grow older they get the message that they are just no good at it. So they stop drawing completely. I really don't know why that is."

Mark relates a story about his early bookmaking endeavors. Recently, while cleaning out the attic, his mother came across a pile of books he'd made as a child. Mark had the opportunity to look them over. He reports, "I don't think if you looked at these books you'd say, 'Oh, here's a future artist.' It's just typical kids' stuff."

The stories featured, oddly enough, a great number of frogs— but not ordinary, pond-dwelling amphibians. Mark's frogs were swashbuckling adventurers—frog pirates, frog detectives, frog flying aces. Mark claims to have no idea where his fascination with frogs, er, *leaped* from, but he does admit this: "My daughter Lily shares this obsession with frogs, and I swear I didn't put her up to it." He muses, "I guess there's a genetic link in there, a frog-appreciation gene that's been passed along."

After college, Mark found himself at loose ends. The end of a long road trip landed him in New York City, working in the display department of a Barnes & Noble bookstore. At Barnes & Noble, Mark rediscovered children's books and was particularly excited by the elaborate paintings of artists like Chris Van Allsburg and William Joyce. He recalls, "It

reminded me of how much I had enjoyed picture books as a child—and how much fun it had been to write and illustrate my own stories at that age."

> ***"I think visually. No matter what I'm reading, it translates into a movie in my mind. If I like the movie, then I feel I can illustrate it."***

Mark got right to work, writing and illustrating his first book. He confesses, "I had no idea about the business end of it, or what the odds were. I just sort of proceeded with the notion that it was something I could do." He modestly concludes, "That's what youth is for—you can be dumb enough to try things like that!"

In Mark's many books, anything can—and often does—happen. His books are gleefully inventive, combining ordinary events of childhood with rich, dreamlike fantasy. Mark appreciates that young readers seem happy, willing, and able to enter his imaginative realms. Mark says, "I do think that kids respond to it, and I'm happy to work that vein. I like absurdity, and there's plenty of it around."

Mark is wary of dissecting his creative process. He confesses, "Who really knows where ideas come from? What's hard about

talking about writing or artwork is you're trying to describe with the rational part of your brain this process that takes place in some part of your mind you don't really have access to."

Nevertheless, Mark has uncovered some clues in old journals and sketchbooks. "I write lists," Mark says, "just free writing, whatever comes to mind. Sometimes I look at old notebooks to see what ideas have been stranded there over time. I've noticed that I'll often find in notebooks, three or four years before the story is written, the birth of the idea in one of these lists.

"For instance, years and years ago, in a really old notebook, I found in one of these lists the word *pigsty*. It never came off the list. I never took it out and played with it or anything. But it was there. In a later notebook there was a little bit more evidence of me trying to work it out: *Pigsty/messy bedroom/ problems?* Clearly I was messing around with it. But again it didn't come. And when it did finally come, the story came fluidly and easily. Clearly, on some level, I think I was working on the story for years."

DO IT YOURSELF!

Talk to Mark Teague about writing and drawing, and the word *free* comes up often. That's how Mark lets his imagination flow—he draws and writes freely, especially in the beginning, just following whatever flights of fancy strike his mind. Only later, in revision, does Mark cut and trim and rework ideas. Try it yourself. Make a strange list. Fill a page of doodles. Don't worry about whether it's good or not. Just let the ideas flow.

Chris Van Allsburg

Born: June 18, 1949, in Grand Rapids, Michigan
Home: Providence, Rhode Island

SELECTED TITLES

The Garden of Abdul Gasazi
(Caldecott Honor Book)
1979

Jumanji
(Caldecott Medal)
1981

The Wreck of the Zephyr
1983

The Mysteries of Harris Burdick
1984

The Polar Express
(Caldecott Medal)
1985

The Stranger
1986

The Z Was Zapped: A Play in Twenty-Six Acts
1987

Just a Dream
1990

The Widow's Broom
1992

The Sweetest Fig
1993

Bad Day at Riverbend
1995

A boy in bed floats high above the treetops. A sailboat lifts off the water and flies among the clouds. And on a snowy winter's night, a train mysteriously pauses on a quiet street.

Welcome to the world of Chris Van Allsburg—a world of mystery, magic, and strange beauty. It is a world where, in Chris's words, "strange things may happen."

Though Chris doesn't know where his ideas come from, he does admit that his stories usually evolve from a single illustration. He says, "I start with an image, and I know there must be a story that makes sense of it."

Try to imagine Chris Van Allsburg working in his large studio in Providence, Rhode Island. There he is: drawing aimlessly, creating images on paper. Puzzled, he stops to look at the picture in front of him. It may be a haunting illustration of a train in front of a house. Somehow, the picture creates questions in Chris's mind. How did the train get there? Where is it going? Why?

At that exact moment—when Chris begins to ask questions—the process of creating the story begins. He becomes an explorer, searching for answers. Only a story can solve the mystery of a picture's strange, new world.

Van Allsburg remarks, "It almost seems like a discovery, as if the story was always there. The few elements I start out with are actually clues. If I figure out what they mean, I can discover the story that's waiting."

That process is exactly how Chris "discovered" *The Polar Express*. He thought about the boy and the train. In his imagination, he got on the train to see where it would lead him. He recalls, "The train kept rolling all the way to the North Pole."

Like Making Movies

Chris Van Allsburg was already a successful sculptor when he began writing and illustrating books for children. Oddly enough, it all happened because he didn't want to watch TV. Chris remembers, "I began drawing little pictures—it was either that or watch TV. My wife thought they'd appeal to kids. I wrote a little story, and that became my first book."

"I'm pleased when my own drawings are a little mysterious to me. I like to create a world where not everything is possible, but where strange things may happen."

Sound easy? It isn't. Chris says, "A book is a four-and-a-half-month commitment, and the challenge is to actually finish it." One of Chris's problems is that he gets too many ideas. He confesses, "I've got a sketchbook in my head with thousands of pieces of sculpture and enough descriptions for ten books. I would like to be six people at once, so that I could get more of them out of the way."

Many critics believe that Chris Van Allsburg is one of the most

technically accomplished illustrators today. He works very hard to make his pictures exciting. Chris believes that making a book is a lot like making a movie. The illustrator is like the director—the person who decides where to place the camera. When you look at Chris's illustrations, think about where he "places the camera" for each scene. Sometimes the camera, or point of view, is very close to a character; other times the camera may be up in the clouds, looking down upon a wide landscape. The camera changes position often, making the story dramatic and lively.

Chris explains, "After I have the text and know essentially what has to be illustrated, I'll do a lot of crude thumbnail sketches that deal with point of view.

"The truth is, there are many ways to do an illustration. In terms of point of view and lighting alone, there are an infinite number of possibilities. Through sketching, I narrow my choices."

DO IT YOURSELF!

Make a viewfinder out of a square of paper. Fold the square in half and cut out a square from the center. Then open the square and look through the opening. To view a scene differently, move the viewfinder closer to or farther from your face. Select an illustration from one of Chris's books and look at it through the viewfinder. Move the viewfinder to focus on one part, or pull back to show more of the surrounding area. Draw several rough sketches of the same illustration, using different perspectives for each.

Bernard Waber

Born: September 27, 1924, in Philadelphia, Pennsylvania
Home: Baldwin Harbor, New York

SELECTED TITLES

The House on East 88th Street
(first in the Lyle series)
1962

Rich Cat, Poor Cat
1963

Just Like Abraham Lincoln
1964

Lyle, Lyle, Crocodile
1965

A Firefly Named Torchy
1970

Ira Sleeps Over
1972

Dear Hildegarde
1980

Bernard
1982

Do You See a Mouse?
1995

A Lion Named Shirley Williamson
1996

The Mouse That Snored
2000

Perhaps the most important aspect of writing, Bernard Waber believes, is *thinking* about writing. "A lot of my books begin with ideas that amuse me, but that's just the starting point," Waber explains. "The nice thing about humor is that after you have an idea that you think is humorous, there is always another side that's sad and complicated. Those are the things you discover after you start writing."

The story *Ira Sleeps Over*, for example, began with a simple idea: A boy is torn between the comfort of his teddy bear and his desire to go to a sleepover. But gradually, by writing and thinking about the idea, new dimensions of the story began to emerge for Waber. He says, "If you work hard on something, and think about it very deeply, new ideas sort of bubble to the surface."

That's why revising—which literally means "to see again"—is so important. While revising, the author has the opportunity to take a new look at the story. Bernard Waber understands it this way: "I find that while rewriting—even just retyping a page—new things come in that I hadn't thought about before. Rewriting is important. I don't think you are finished after only one or two drafts. Rewriting is not only polishing sentences; it is also a process of searching for new things to improve your story."

Without rewriting, Waber could not have written *Ira Sleeps Over*—one of his best-loved books. Bernard wrote a first version of *Ira Sleeps Over*, which no one besides his editor has ever seen. "I sent in an early version to my publisher," Waber recalls. "I thought I had finished with it. Then an entirely different writing style just suddenly popped into my head. I rewrote the story entirely. Then I got a call from my editor. She said that she pretty much liked the first version. But I said, 'Well, actually, I have a second version for you.'" The second version was even better. It became the published version that readers know and love.

The Youngest in the Family

Bernard Waber grew up in a household with two older brothers and an older sister. He reflects, "It's taken me a long time to realize the richness I had. Nowadays, I finally understand how much I got from my siblings. They were very artistic. I had a brother who loved literature and chess; I suppose he passed that on to me. I had another brother who liked to write and draw. My sister played piano. She even wrote love letters for her friends, like Cyrano de Bergerac!"

"You want to write from the heart, that's the important thing."

The youngest child in a creative family, Bernard found plenty of time to daydream. "I lived a fantasy life," he said. Part of that life involved going to the movies and staying all day long. He would sit in the theater and watch the same movie over and over again, until one of his parents finally arrived to drag him home.

Like many artists who both write and illustrate, Waber finds that his dual roles make him feel slightly schizophrenic. "When I am writing, I think of myself as a writer. But when I am illustrating, I think of myself as an illustrator. I think, though, that I try to create situations with my writing that will be fun to illustrate. The writer in me tries to please the illustrator."

Almost all writers aspire to give up their "regular" jobs to become full-time writers. But not Bernard Waber. He liked his regular job too much. (Waber worked as a graphic designer on *Life* and *People* magazines into the late 1980s.) Waber thinks that having a full-time job actually may have helped his writing: "Having another job gave me artistic freedom; I didn't have to worry about making money through my books. I was able to write whatever I wanted to."

Bernard Waber enjoys visiting children in schools across the country. The part he enjoys most, he says, is talking with fellow writers. "These days, with so many children writing their own stories, it's interesting to talk to them about writing. They ask thoughtful questions about where ideas come from and the various stages of writing. I'm very impressed with their knowledge."

DO IT YOURSELF!

"Kids enjoy writing their own Lyle stories," Bernard Waber says. "Lyle Goes to School, Lyle Plays Ice Hockey, or even Lyle Gets Married." What would happen if one day a friendly crocodile joined your classroom? How would your teacher react? How would your classmates react? Write your own Lyle story.

Kate Waters

Born: September 4, 1951, in Rochester, New York
Home: New York, New York

Books have always been at the center of Kate Waters's life. The oldest of six children in a lively (but noisy!) household, Kate knew that she could find solace by retreating into the world of books. Kate recalls, "The first time I heard my mother say, 'Shh, leave Katie alone. She's reading,' I realized that reading would not only take me to other worlds, it would also give me some peace and quiet for a few minutes!"

Kate recalls her childhood with great affection. "My mother read to us every day. She made the magical world of Narnia and *The Borrowers* come alive. I learned about storytelling from my father, who explained the constellations, the causes of fog, how sap changes into maple syrup, and what a starfish is."

It was surely no surprise when, as an adult, Kate became a children's librarian. Later Kate continued working with books, both as a teacher of children's literature and an editor. It was only a matter of time, perhaps, before Kate decided to write a book of her own.

It happened, strangely, because Kate wasn't satisfied with the books she'd been reading. In particular,

Kate became increasingly frustrated by many books on Pilgrim life in America. "I was beginning to see more and more false stereotypes—mostly in the illustrations," Kate recalls. "As one small example, in many pictures we see Pilgrims wearing black clothes, with a square hat and a buckle. But buckles had not even been invented! They were not used on clothes until 1726—and we're talking about 1620."

Because nothing offends a librarian so much as misinformation, she set out to provide a more accurate account of Pilgrim life. Kate also came up with a unique idea. She wanted to use photography! Kate explains, "I remembered visiting Plimoth Plantation when I lived in Boston. I suggested to my editor that we take photographs there. The photographs let people see what life was like for those first

Europeans who settled in New England."

Kate had something deeper in mind as well. She wanted to make history much more than a tired list of facts and dates. By focusing on an individual—like Sarah Morton, Samuel Eaton, or the Wampanoag Indian boy, Tapenum—Kate strives to help children connect with history. She observes, "People in history—far from being dry and boring—are interesting if you can find the parts of them that are like you."

"When I do my research, I often feel as if the people I'm reading about are standing over my shoulder, whispering 'Tell our story right. Here's another clue.'"

Kate contends that in many ways, people throughout history remain fundamentally unchanged. She explains, "Your soul, your hopes, your dreams, your fears—those things haven't changed much for people throughout time."

Of course, long months of research lie at the heart of Kate's work. But for Kate, research offers the thrill of a great mystery. She becomes like a detective, seeking clues: "I read all the primary source material I can find," Kate explains. "I try to answer the

questions: What was life like then? What were this child's hopes and dreams? How was this child like children today?"

With eight books written and more on the way (Kate plans a fresh, historically accurate look at the harvest feast commonly known as the first Thanksgiving), Waters still feels drawn to the time when Europeans first set sail for North America. She explains her fascination, with a mixture of awe and respect: "I admire that they had the nerve to act on a dream. To me, that's why the *Mayflower* is an icon of this country. These folks, in an effort to live in a way they were convinced they needed to live, got on a ship and went to a place they'd never seen before. Nobody on that ship had ever seen North America—including all the crew and the captain. They went to a place they had never seen in pursuit of a dream. That's courage."

Sarah Morton's Day

A Day in the Life of a Pilgrim Girl

by KATE WATERS

Photographs by RUSS KENDALL

DO IT YOURSELF!

Kate Waters finds herself returning to the same favorite books over and over. She explains, "It refreshes my mind as to what makes good writing. Why have these books lived for me for so long? What does the author do? How can I pick it apart to figure out how they did this?" It's a valuable exercise, since careful reading is at the heart of good writing. Kate suggests, "If you have a favorite author, try to figure out what that author does. How does he make a world real to you? How does a mystery author make you sit on the edge of your seat? Puzzling over how authors craft their books will help you become a better writer."

Rosemary Wells

Born: January 29, 1943, in New York, New York
Home: Briarcliff Manor, New York

Though Rosemary Wells is both a writer and an illustrator, she firmly believes that the story is the central part of a good picture book. "The misconception is that it is relatively easy to write for children, that illustrating is the hard part. I believe the opposite is true," she states. "The words come first. The story begins with feelings and is embellished with humor, adventure, and character. The words it takes to bring these elements to life are paramount. When they are truly well done, the book becomes poetry."

According to Rosemary, writing for children is much more difficult than writing for adults. The main reason: A children's book must remain enjoyable even after it has been read aloud five hundred times! Rosemary states, "Writing for young children is the rarest voice in all literature."

Beginning With Emotions

To create her stories, Rosemary often draws upon episodes in her own life and the lives of her two daughters, Victoria and Meg. A family pet and his heirs also play important roles. Rosemary explains, "Our West Highland white terrier, Angus, had the shape and expressions to become Benjamin, Tulip, and Timothy, and all the other animals I have made up for my stories. He also appears as himself in a couple of books."

Although Rosemary will sometimes get an idea from observing her own children, she believes that "it's much more important to have been a child than to have children. It's because I was a child and I'm very close to that time in my life that I can do this. Incidents from childhood are universal."

While she stresses that each book has a logic of its own—"there is no single way of doing it"—Rosemary usually begins by focusing on one particular character. "The central issue in all my books is emotional content," she says. "I continually pick similar themes. One of the themes I use a lot is belonging to a group or feeling that you don't belong."

> **"Writing for children is as difficult as writing serious verse. Writing for children is as mysterious as writing fine music. It is as personal as singing."**

Like most writers, Rosemary takes small incidents—a snatch of overheard conversation, a long-held memory, an amusing thought—and runs them through to their logical conclusions in her mind.

Rosemary gives an example: "When my daughter Beezoo was in second grade, she wanted more than anything to take in her favorite stuffed animal for show-and-tell. She decided against it at the last minute, however, because, as she put it, 'The boys would rip it up.'" With that insight in mind, Rosemary wrote *Hazel's Amazing Mother*.

"The thing that fiction writers do, of course, is change everything," Rosemary confesses. "We don't write things up as case histories. You change it, reduce it, or embellish it to make the story better.

"Three-quarters of all writing is revising," Rosemary believes. "It's tremendously important to work hard, to practice, and to revise—to do things again and again and again until they are right. You can't just snap it out and say it's going to be right the first time. It isn't right," she says matter-of-factly, "until it's right.

"When I go to workshops for young writers, I bring a kaleidoscope with a detachable end, but I don't tell them it's a kaleidoscope at first," Rosemary explains. "Then I show them a handful of junk—paper clips, little plastic files, a couple of buttons—the kind of stuff you might find at the bottom of a drawer and throw out. I tell them that when you put all these different shapes and colors into the kaleidoscope, and you hold it up to your eyes, you make a rose window."

Rosemary pauses a moment before making her point: "Everybody makes a different window," she says. "You turn the kaleidoscope and the exact image can never be repeated again. The design is yours to make from the ordinary essence of life. That's what writing is about. Very ordinary things become a rose window if you organize them and you let yourself think about it. Without writing, without writing well, we cannot convey many ideas. And without ideas," Rosemary concludes, "we become drones."

ROSEMARY WELLS
Hazel's Amazing Mother

DO IT YOURSELF!

Rosemary Wells offers this suggestion to children: "Increase your vocabulary, because increasing vocabulary means increasing thought. Never forget that English is by far the biggest language in the world. If you doubt this, look up in your thesaurus how many synonyms there are for, say, the word *pleasant*. The more words you know, and the more words you can use, the more profoundly you can think for yourself." So the next time you read a word you don't know, pick up a dictionary and find out what it means.

Hans Wilhelm

Born: September 21, 1945, in Bremen, Germany
Home: Westport, Connecticut

SELECTED TITLES

Bunny Trouble
1985

I'll Always Love You
1985

Let's Be Friends Again!
1986

Oh, What a Mess
1988

Tyrone the Horrible
1988

The Bremen Town Musicians
1992

The Boy Who Wasn't There
1993

The Royal Raven
1996

Don't Cut My Hair
1997

I Love Colors!
2000

Hans Wilhelm believes that a book is, at its heart, a sharing of emotions. "Just as a letter is a very personal thing," he explains, "so is a book."

Hans continues, "The basic emotion in the book must be something that is also in me. So I must come in touch with that problem. I don't believe there are solely childhood problems. The fear of rejection, loneliness, sibling rivalry, dealing with a bully—you don't outgrow these things as an adult. I think all of our feelings are the same."

One of Hans's most famous books, *I'll Always Love You*, illustrates his point about the importance of true emotion in writing. It is the story of a friendship between a young boy and his dog, Elfie. With charming, often humorous pictures and very few words, Hans shows how the boy and the dog grow up together. As the boy gets bigger and stronger, the dog grows older and weaker. Eventually, as would happen in real life, Elfie dies.

Hans confesses, "*I'll Always Love You* is autobiographical. The dog in my life was called Elfie. I wrote that book years later, long after Elfie died." In order to write the book, Hans had to remember his childhood feelings: the love he felt, and the sadness he endured. Readers don't have to own a dog to appreciate the story, however. It is about a universal feeling that everyone encounters at one time or another. Hans says, "I think that book relates not only to animals but to human beings as well. It could be about losing a parent or a friend. I think readers sense this."

Hans offers this advice to young writers and illustrators: "You cannot be afraid of showing your true self if you wish to become an author or illustrator of books. Each page and each word can reveal your emotions and fears."

Real Emotions

Hans Wilhelm sits down at his table and begins the workday bright and early. He says, "I am a morning person, so that's the best time for me to have creative ideas

and thoughts. Therefore, I write and illustrate in the morning and use the afternoon for the administrative part of my work." Hans usually works in his studio in Connecticut, but he keeps another studio in his native Germany.

- -

"I think that a children's book is an adult book that is so good it even satisfies children."

- -

Hans believes that working on a story is a process of discovery. While writing and sketching, he tries to stay open to new ideas as they occur. "Once I see the characters on my sheet of paper, they begin to communicate with me and often they develop quite differently from what I originally had in mind. I always allow for fun and surprises as I work on a story."

Hans gets his ideas by using his imagination, his dreams, and experiences from his own life. He also stresses the importance of listening. Just quietly listening, Hans tells us, is a wonderful way to discover ideas. "Many things we hear or read are so incredible that they make wonderful stories!"

Hans grew up in Bremen, Germany. He recalls, "Some of my favorite memories are of climbing trees, building tree houses, and watching wild animals." As a child, Hans always wrote and illustrated

his own stories just for fun.

When Hans first came to the United States many years ago, he had to struggle with the English language. He thinks this made him work harder on his illustrations. "This struggle," Hans says, "forced me to express feelings, fine nuances, and subtleties in my illustrations. The visual does not have language barriers. In my pictures I can converse and say all the things that I wish to communicate." He points out, "The illustrations are a passport to everybody's heart, without any translations!"

With a warm blend of seriousness and humor, Hans Wilhelm's books have offered an enjoyable experience to thousands of children in many different countries. For Hans, it's a dream come true. "I try to have a good time while I'm making a book," he confides. "Even if the process of making a book also means a lot of sweating, the overall experience must also be joyful and positive. I believe that making books is my way of sharing my joy with others."

DO IT YOURSELF!

Hans Wilhelm has said, "A book is basically nothing other than a letter, because it, too, is a sharing of emotions." Write a letter to a friend or a family member. In your letter, write about something—a person, a place, an event—that gave you a special feeling. The emotion could be anything: joy, fear, sadness, love. Then ask yourself, "Is there any way I could turn this letter into a story?"

Vera B. Williams

Born: January 28, 1927, in Hollywood, California
Home: New York, New York

SELECTED TITLES

The Great Watermelon Birthday
1980

Three Days on a River in a Red Canoe
1981

A Chair for My Mother
(Caldecott Honor Book)
1982

Something Special for Me
1983

Music, Music for Everyone
1984

Cherries and Cherry Pits
1986

Stringbean's Trip to the Shining Sea
1988

"More, More, More," Said the Baby
(Caldecott Honor Book)
1990

Lucky Song
1997

"I like to visit schools because I really like hanging around with children," says Vera Williams. When Vera visits a classroom, she tries to help children understand how a book is made. She says, "I try to turn the whole thing into an example of what I do. Sometimes when I visit, I put tape over my mouth and don't speak at all. I just start to draw. Then I take the tape off my mouth and say, 'Well, that's me as an illustrator—drawing is one way of talking.' And if I make mistakes, which of course I do, I get the children to play editor. I say, 'Well, you see, I don't hand it to you perfect!'"

Vera enjoys children because they give her the chance to be playful. She also enjoys the questions they ask. She says, "They ask things like 'Do you have a limousine?' or 'How come you're so old?'" Vera laughs, "That's easy to answer—I was born in 1927!"

When illustrating in front of children, Vera often likes to examine what makes a face seem more like a girl's or a boy's. She says, "I'd draw this face. At first, I'd just draw this empty thing. Sometimes I'd joke: 'Is it a boy or a girl?' They'd yell 'Boy!' or 'Girl!'

Meanwhile, there were no features at all. So I'd say, 'Don't be silly, it's a potato!'"

What has Vera learned from her experiments with gender stereotypes? "Short hair always makes it a boy," she says, "even when there are girls in the classroom with short haircuts. Heart-shaped faces are thought to be female, while long, square faces are male. It's very complicated.

"For instance, as soon as I put eyelashes on a drawing they all yell, 'It's a girl!' Then I have to ask them if boys come without eyelashes. This always ends in a lot of laughter and, I trust, some new thoughts."

Growing up, Vera and her older sister, Naomi, were encouraged to express their creative talents. On Saturdays

they traveled together on the subway to attend art classes. In high school Vera wrote and illustrated her first book, which was about a gigantic banana.

"I've always had the feeling, even from childhood, that lettering, text, and pictures are very closely related."

The emotions and experiences of childhood continue to play an important role in Vera's work. "When I first started doing my books for children, I tried to remember the pictures from my own childhood, how I did them, what I was feeling when I made them."

Vera confides, "Many of my illustrations appear to have been dashed off—and so they were, some of them over and over. Sometimes I select one entire drawing from a number of attempts; sometimes I cut and paste parts from various drawings."

Because Vera does so much revision, she admits, "I don't have such good work habits when it comes to getting things done quickly. I am not content with my first, second, or third solutions. I do incredible numbers of sketches. I just have to draw and draw and draw until I get it right."

Writing on Postcards

Vera B. Williams
A CHAIR FOR MY MOTHER

Usually, Vera begins the creative process by thinking about and writing down the story. The illustrations come later. But that wasn't the case with *Stringbean's Trip to the Shining Sea*. "For that book," Vera says, "I never really wrote a story.

"No typed manuscript exists for that book—I wrote it on postcards, because the book has a postcard style," Vera says. "So it wasn't written and then translated to postcards; it actually consists of postcards that I made up as I went along. I tried to work in such a way that the process and the outcome would be one." Writing on postcards, Vera Williams noticed, was very different from regular writing. She explains, "On postcards we tend to drop off the subject of the sentence. Ordinarily you'd say, 'I went to the Grand Canyon yesterday.' But a lot of postcards start, 'Went to Grand Canyon.' You do absolutely anything to save space."

DO IT YOURSELF!

Try, as Vera Williams did, to tell a story by writing a series of postcards. Get some blank index cards. Draw pictures on one side and write on the other. Create a story about a trip to a strange, new land.

Jane Yolen

Born: February 11, 1939, in New York, New York
Home: Hatfield, Massachusetts

Readers frequently ask Jane Yolen, "Where do you get your great ideas?" But there really isn't a satisfactory answer to that question because most authors don't honestly know where their ideas come from. For that reason, perhaps it's better to ask, "What do you do with your ideas once you get them?" Now that's a question Jane Yolen can sink her teeth into.

"I keep an idea file," she says. "I always scribble down ideas when I get them. I find that so many ideas come to me that if I don't write them down, they're gone.

"I have one whole file-cabinet drawer filled with file folders that have maybe a paragraph, two paragraphs, or a page or two of this new idea. Whenever I've reached a point with my other work—that either nothing's going well or I've finished some major project—I go and look through all those files to see if there's anything that says, 'Me! It's my turn, I'm ready. I want to be the next story.'"

But ideas don't become books overnight. It's a gradual process that sometimes takes several years. Jane offers an example: "I had been writing poems about cats, not knowing what to do with them. I was thinking maybe, eventually, I'd have a book of cat poems. But something was not there. I had been writing these poems for maybe eight years. And then one day the phrase *raining cats and dogs* came to me. And I said, I'm going to write a book of cats *and* dogs. It's going to be called *Raining Cats and Dogs*. With that incentive, I wrote some dog poems to match the cat poems. So you see, that's an idea that moved along over many years."

The Sound of Words

As a writer, Jane is drawn to magical or mythological subjects. Strange events occur in her stories: A girl cries flowers; a boy learns how to fly; a deer turns into a unicorn. In Jane's hands even a realistic story such as *Owl Moon* conveys a mood of magic, mystery, and wonder.

Perhaps the biggest influence on

Yolen's writing has been the oral tradition of storytellers. The sound of the words is very important to her. "I read everything out loud. So I think, instead of seeing pictures, I am hearing the story as music." She believes that it is important for young writers to try to write every day. It's also important to realize that every writer gets rejections—even writers with well over one hundred books published, like Jane Yolen.

> **"I've always felt that the audience I'm writing for is myself—the child that I was and the child who is still inside me."**

"I got one last week," Jane admits. "That's fine. Because a rejection doesn't mean that you're no good, and it doesn't necessarily mean that the piece is no good: It means that one person didn't like it. One person. My way of dealing with rejections is to get angry for about a minute and a half and then send the manuscript out again."

Yolen also spends a good part of her time speaking out against censorship. Censorship stems from the word *censure*, which means "to criticize severely." When books are censored, they are kept out of classrooms and libraries. For example, some people believe that children should not be allowed to read

books or see movies that have witches in them. Jane Yolen disagrees: "To say that you can't have children see *The Wizard of Oz* because there are witches in it is absolutely ridiculous."

Yolen believes that many people who favor censorship misunderstand literature. "I think that the people who are most involved in censorship—especially of fantasy books—have no sense of metaphor. If you don't have a sense of metaphor, then you begin to believe these things are absolutely point-for-point true, in the small sense, the lowercase *t*.

"I think fantasy books and metaphor teach us about Truth with a capital *T*. They are talking about love, honor, loyalty, and bravery—not about witchcraft!"

Jane Yolen offers this advice to aspiring writers: "It's important to keep open your sense of wonder, your sense of curiosity, your sense of exploration. I think good writers have to be in touch with that openness—that willingness to be surprised."

OWL MOON

by Jane Yolen
illustrated by John Schoenherr

DO IT YOURSELF!

Jane Yolen sometimes invents stories by beginning with a situation and asking herself, "What next?" Try it yourself. The situation can be anything: A cow falls in love with a frog or a spaceship lands in your backyard. Ask yourself, "What happens next?" The answer you come up with is an idea for a story you could write!

Ed Young

Born: November 28, 1931, in Tientsin, China
Home: Hastings-on-Hudson, New York

SELECTED TITLES

The Emperor and the Kite
(Caldecott Honor Book)
1967

Yeh-Shen: A Cinderella Story From China
1982

The Double Life of Pocahontas
1983

Foolish Rabbit's Big Mistake
1985

In the Night, Still Dark
1988

Lon Po Po: A Red-Riding Hood Story From China
(Caldecott Medal)
1989

Dreamcatcher
1992

Seven Blind Mice
(Caldecott Honor Book)
1992

Night Visitors
1995

The Lost Horse
1998

The Hunter
2000

Caldecott Medal–winning illustrator Ed Young doesn't like to overemphasize the process of creativity. He says, "To me, it is the attitude behind everything that is more important than the procedure."

A deeply thoughtful man, Ed Young believes that the creation of art involves much more than technical skill. Drawing and writing, he says, "are expressions of the inner rather than the outer person."

In practicing calligraphy, Young refined his brush strokes and achieved a greater sensitivity to his craft. In calligraphy, as in life, Young believes that attitude is of prime importance. "A person has to know the nature of a brush, the nature of ink in the brush, the nature of ink applied by the brush onto paper. That person has to be friends with all of these in order to see what the brush is capable of doing.

"It is like training a horse. A person has to know what the nature of the horse is in order to ride it correctly. If the horse knows that the person understands him and gives him every possibility of exploring his potential, the horse will be very happy. And so with the brush."

Exploring With Pencil

Once he has selected a manuscript, Young begins by making a series of sketches. The process is similar to an exploration; with each sketch, Young searches for the proper tone and image for the story. He says, "First I do little thumbnails right on the margin of the manuscript whenever there is a picture that comes to me. I just scribble, and the pictures that I draw are no more than maybe a half or three-quarters of an inch. It's just a record of images that are in my head."

In what he calls "rounds," Young revisits his initial sketches and expands upon them. Slowly, he adds more details and the tiny pictures grow larger. Young explains, "They graduate, let's say, from the first set of very small thumbnails to something two or three inches tall by five or six inches wide. At

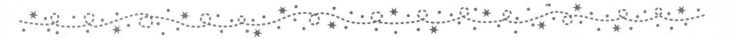

that point I start to go into the characters or buildings or costumes, that kind of thing."

> **"I have never lost the child in me. I think everyone has a child in him who responds to anything that has true meaning."**

During the next round, research becomes very important. In the first sketches, Young seeks to capture a general impression, a feeling. Next, he strives for painstaking accuracy. The pictures themselves seem to ask him these questions: In what style should the characters be dressed? What are the trees and flowers like in that part of the world? What is the style of architecture?

To achieve this level of accuracy, Young turns to magazines, books, libraries, museums, or wherever he can find the information he needs. Young goes to all this trouble because he feels that factual detail helps create a believable fantasy. As an artist, he is preparing an imaginative world for the reader to visit. The trees, the flowers, the buildings—every last *thing*—must be true to that world.

An example of Young's emphasis on detail can be found in the work he did for *Lon Po Po*. The story, which is a Chinese version of "Little Red Riding Hood," involves a wolf and children. (*Lon Po Po* means "Granny Wolf" in Chinese.) Ed Young explains how he made the wolf and children believable. "I drew a whole series on how wolves communicate with each other, using their ears, their tails, and the way they hold themselves. That had to be right because the wolf talks to the children in the story, so he has to be alive to them. Then I had to know how the children talked to each other, how they lived in the compound, how the trees would grow. Once you know everything about the story, you can express it in fresh ways."

Ed Young grew up in Shanghai and later moved to Hong Kong before eventually settling in the United States. Of his childhood, Young recalls: "Our summer nights were usually spent on the flat roof of the three-story house that my father designed. Against the background of crickets chirping in the starry night, my father would spin endless tales of his own to entertain our imagination until the heat finally subsided. I have never forgotten the images I saw in my mind as I listened."

DO IT YOURSELF!

Ed Young thinks that kids who like to draw should make up their own illustrations to go with their favorite stories. Why not try it? Your own pictures will help you tell the story the way you see it. "There are things," he says, "that pictures can do that words never can."

Charlotte Zolotow

Born: June 26, 1915, in Norfolk, Virginia
Home: Hastings-on-Hudson, New York

SELECTED TITLES

The Storm Book
(Caldecott Honor Book)
1952

*Mr. Rabbit and the
Lovely Present*
(Caldecott Honor Book)
1962

*The Poodle Who Barked
at the Wind*
1964

Big Sister and Little Sister
1966

William's Doll
1972

May I Visit?
1976

Someone New
1978

If You Listen
1980

I Know a Lady
1984

*Everything Glistens and
Everything Sings*
1987

This Quiet Lady
1992

Sleepy Book
2001

The author of more than 70 books for children, Charlotte Zolotow explores the ordinary emotions that touch a child's life. Yet her writing is anything but ordinary. With an artist's eye for detail, Charlotte is a poet of the everyday—capturing the emotions that bring us together and the events that define our lives.

Many of Charlotte's books are like illustrated poems—quiet, reflective, heartfelt. It is a great pleasure to listen to her stories read aloud. The flow of words seems to wash over the reader like soothing waves. Her books are often based on feelings or moods she may have experienced. Writing with sensitivity and grace, Charlotte explores the twists and turns of her own meandering heart. She recalls the comment of legendary children's book editor Ursula Nordstrom, who said: "Everybody who writes children's books should have a direct line to his or her own childhood."

Charlotte explains, "All of my books are based on an adult emotion that connects with a similar emotion that I had as a child. I like each of my books for a different reason, because each comes out of a different emotion.

If a book succeeds in bringing an emotion into focus, then I like that book very much."

Missing a Friend or Father

In the book *If You Listen* a young girl misses her father. Charlotte says that this feeling—missing an absent friend—is one she has experienced many times as an adult. She adds, "Also, as a child, my father traveled a lot and I was very fond of him. I can remember sitting there and thinking about him, knowing that somewhere he was out there and he was coming back to me."

Now read this passage taken from *If You Listen*. Notice how Charlotte uses a small detail, the bird, to fill the moment with feeling: *The little girl sat still a long time. She was*

thinking of her father. She looked up at the sky. It was a clear blue. One bird circled and circled overhead. She watched until he flew away.

"Things that matter to children—that's what I try to get into my books. Things that are very important, even if they aren't important to the adults around them."

Charlotte, who worked as a children's book editor for many years, enjoys going on solitary walks by the Hudson River. This is her chance to be quiet, to watch the world, to be refreshed by nature. Charlotte says, "You just let your mind go free and then out of it things fall into place."

Ideas, for Charlotte, come at these private times. She may be overcome by a mood or an emotion. The stories, it seems, come from her heart rather than her head. Charlotte explains: "When you're washing dishes or doing any manual task—when you're thinking that you're not thinking—that is the time when things really begin to take shape."

Charlotte begins the writing process by trying to capture the feeling. "Often with writing," says the author, "you begin by writing too much. And out of it suddenly emerges one line that's exactly right. That one line reveals the essence of the story. It's a strange process that's almost impossible to describe."

During revision, Charlotte reads her manuscript aloud. She says, "I find that I might write pages of description—I love to write description—and then rereading it, I see how I could set the mood in three sentences rather than three pages. So I do a great deal of cutting back." Almost with a sense of wonder, Charlotte adds, "With some manuscripts revision takes forever, while with others it just sort of happens . . . magically."

When speaking with Charlotte Zolotow, one idea comes up again and again: Write from the heart. Charlotte says, "I don't think children should be marked on spelling, or at least if they are marked, it should be separate from content. When you try to teach someone how to write, what you should say is: 'Put down your thoughts. Put down the things that are hard to say, the things that you want to say.' Then let that student be judged on the content, on how honest he or she is."

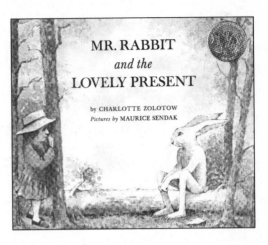

MR. RABBIT and the LOVELY PRESENT
by CHARLOTTE ZOLOTOW
Pictures by MAURICE SENDAK

DO IT YOURSELF!

Charlotte recommends this simple writing exercise: "Write a line about feeling sad, mad, bad, or glad—something you really feel. Give examples of incidents that have made you feel that way. Some of these examples might make a good book or two!"

Bibliography

Almost all of the material in this book was obtained through direct interviews with the authors and illustrators. In many cases, however, additional biographical information was supplied by their publishers or found in relevant books and articles. The Something About the Author series (Gale Research) was an especially helpful resource.

Allender, David. "William Steig at 80." *Publishers Weekly*, July 24, 1987.

"Allen Say." A Scholastic Author Tape, Scholastic, 1992.

Allis, Sam. "Rhinoceroses in the Living Room." *Time*, November 13, 1989.

Anno, Mitsumasa. "Why I Write and Paint." Transcription of speech as interpreted by Tadatoshi Akiba, n.d.

Antonucci, Ron. "Rylant on Writing." *School Library Journal*, May 1993.

Aoki, Hisako. "A Conversation with Mitsumasa Anno." *Horn Book*, April 1983.

"Arnold Lobel: The Natural Illustrator, the Entertainer." *Early Years*, November 1980.

Bader, Barbara. "Lionni x 2." *Horn Book*, May/June 1998.

Bandler, Michael J. "Seuss on the Loose." *Parents*, September 1987.

"Barbara Cooney" The Trumpet Club Authors on Tape, Bantam, 1989.

"Bernard Waber." The Trumpet Club Authors on Tape, Bantam, 1989.

Berry, Mary. "Angela Shelf Medearis." *Emergency Librarian*, May/June 1998.

"Bill Martin, Jr. and John Archambault," The Trumpet Club Authors on Tape, Bantam, 1990.

Brainard, Dulcy. "PW Interviews Aliki Brandenberg." *Publishers Weekly*, July 22, 1983.

———. "PW Interviews Ed Young." *Publishers Weekly*, February 24, 1989.

Brandenberg, Aliki. "A Letter to the Class from Aliki." Trumpet Book Club, n.d.

Bridwell, Norman. "Interview Transcript." Scholatsic.com, n.d.

Bryan, Ashley. "On Poetry and Black American Poets." *Horn Book*, February 1979.

Carle, Eric, "Where Do Ideas Come From?" Transcription of speech given at the Library of Congress, n.d.

Christopher, Rita. "A Child at Play." *Maclean's*, June 22, 1981.

Christy, Marian. "A Muse on the Loose." *The Boston Globe*, July 20, 1980.

Clemons, Walter. "Sailboats That Fly and a Train out of Nowhere." *Newsweek*, December 9, 1985.

Crichton, Jennifer. "Dr. Seuss Turns 80." *Publishers Weekly*, February 10, 1984.

"A Conversation with Ezra Jack Keats." Biographical Material, Macmillan, n.d.

Davis, Andrea R. "Pinkney: Illustrating the Point." *American Vision*, April 1989.

Davis, Patricia. "Kindergarten Superstar." *Report on Business Magazine*, December 1989.

Davis, William A. "Author Faces His Toughest Critics: Kids." *The Boston Globe*, November 6, 1990.

dePaola, Tomie. "Involved with Dreams." *Books for Your Children*, Summer 1980.

Dillon, Diane. "Leo Dillon." *Horn Book*, August 1977.

Dillon, Leo. "Diane Dillon." *Horn Book*, August 1977.

———. "Leo and Diane Dillon." *Horn Book*, August 1977.

Dillon, Leo and Diane. "Caldecott Award Acceptance Speech." *Horn Book*, August 1977.

Dingus, Anne. "Angela Shelf Medearis." *Texas Monthly*, September 1997.

"Doubleday Presents Joanna Cole." Biographical Material, Doubleday. n.d.

Dowling, Claudia Gleen. "Dr. Seuss." *Life*, July 1989.

Dummit, Chris. "Still the Cat in the Hat's Meow." *Dallas Morning News*, June 16, 1983.

Edwards, Susan. "A Lot of Untalkable Things." *Vajradhatu Sun*, April–May 1982.

"Ed Young." Scholastic Book Club, n.d.

Elleman, Barbara. "Shonto Begay's The Mud Pony." *Book Links*, July 1992.

Evans, Dily. "Four African American Illustrators," *Book Links*, January 1993.

———. "Leo Lionni." *Book Links*, March 1995.

"Face-to-Face with Eric Carle." *The Follett Forum*, n.d.

"Faith Ringgold." A Scholastic Author Tape, Scholastic, 1993.

Fenly, Leigh. "Artist Lets Dreams of Freedom Take Wing." *The San Diego Union*, February 16, 1991.

Flomenhaft, Eleanor. "Faith Ringgold: A 25 Year Survey." Fine Arts Museums of Long Island, n.d.

Fox, Catherine. "Ringgold's Art Tells Stories, Topples Barriers." *The Atlanta Constitution*, July 30, 1990.

Fox, Mem. *Dear Mem Fox, I Have Read All Your Books Even the Pathetic Ones*. Harcourt Brace Jovanovich, 1992.

Gaither, Edmund B., and Benjamin Peterson. "Interview with Jerry Pinkney." *Massachusetts College of Art*, 1987.

Gaitskell, Susan. "An Interview with Barbara Reid." *Canadian Children's Literature* No. 56, 1989.

———. "Phoebe Gilman." *Canscape Newsletter*, Spring 1986.

Goble, Paul. "On Beaded Dresses and the Blazing Sun," *The Native American Folktale*, 1991.

Gordon, Lucy Latane. "An Interview with Leo Lionni." *Wilson Library Bulletin*, June 1992.

Gorney, Cynthia. "Dr. Seuss." *The*

Washington Post, May 21, 1979.

Hale, Robert. "Musings." *Horn Book*, June 1987.

———. "Musings." *Horn Book*, January/February 1989.

Hearn, Michael Patrick. "Drawing Out William Steig." *Washington Post Book World*, May 11, 1980.

Henkes, Kevin. "The Artist at Work." *Horn Book*, January 1992.

Huston, Margo. "Honesty Is the Author's Policy for Children's Books." *Milwaukee Journal*, March 23, 1974.

Hyman, Trina Schart. "Caldecott Medal Acceptance." *Horn Book*, July/August 1985.

———. *Self-Portrait: Trina Schart Hyman*. Addison-Wesley, 1981.

"An Interview with Ed Young." *Leader Notes*, January-February 1989.

"An Interview with Tomie dePaola." *School Library Media Activities Monthly*, June 1976.

"Introducing Phoebe Gilman." The Canadian Children's Book Center, 1986.

"Introducing Robert Munsch." The Canadian Children's Book Center, 1989.

"James Marshall." The Trumpet Club Authors on Tape, Bantam, 1989.

"Jan Brett." A Scholastic Author Tape, Scholastic, 1991.

"Joanna Cole & Bruce Degen." A Scholastic Author Tape, Scholastic, 1990.

Johnson, Tim. "Dr. Seuss: Architect of Social Change." *Whole Earth Review*, Summer 1988.

"John Steptoe, 1950–1989." Obituary, *Publishers Weekly*, September 29, 1989.

Karlen, Neal. "Yooks and Zooks from Dr. Seuss." *Newsweek*, January 16, 1984.

Keats, Ezra Jack. "Caldecott Award Acceptance." *Horn Book*, August 1963.

———. "Collage." *Horn Book*, June 1964.

Kellogg, Steven. "A Letter to the Class from Steven Kellogg." Trumpet Book Club, n.d

Kroll, Steven. "Steig: Nobody Is Grown-up." *The New York Times Book Review*, June 28, 1987.

Lanes, Selma G. "Ezra Jack Keats: In Memoriam." *Horn Book*, September-October 1984.

———. "A Reformed Masochist Writes a Sunlit Children's Classic." *Harper's*, October 1972.

Laski, Audrey. "Painting with Papers." *London Times*, August 28, 1987.

Levine, Arthur. "Emily Arnold McCully." *Horn Book*, July/August 1993.

Lewis, Valerie. "Meet the Author: Keven Henkes." *Instructor*, September 1994.

———. "Patricia Polacco." *Instructor*, April 1993.

Lobel, Anita. "Arnold at Home." *Horn Book*, August 1981.

Lobel, Arnold. "Caldecott Medal Acceptance Speech." *Horn Book*, August 1981.

"Lois Ehlert." A Scholastic Author Tape, Scholastic, 1992.

Macaulay, David. "Chris Van Allsburg." *Horn Book*, August 1982.

Marantz, Sylvia and Kenneth. "Interview with Ashley Bryan." *Horn Book*, March–April 1988.

Marcus, Leonard. "James Marshall: An Ability to Convey Real Emotions in Ridiculous Situations." *Publishers Weekly*, July 28, 1989.

———. "Travels with Anno." *Parenting*, October 1989.

Marshall, James. "Arnold Lobel." Obituary. *Horn Book*, May–June 1988.

Maughan, Shannon. "Patricia Polacco." *Publishers Weekly*, February 15, 1993.

McCully, Emily Arnold. "Interview Transcript," Scholastic.com, n.d.

McDougall, Carol. "Barbara Reid." *Canscape Newsletter*, Spring 1988.

Meeker, Amy. "Boston Makes Way for Ducklings." *Publishers Weekly*, October 30, 1987.

"Meet the Author: Eric Carle." Scholastic Book Club, n.d.

Meghn, Nick. "The Strength of Weakness: A Profile of Illustrator Jerry Pinkney." *American Artist*, January 1982.

Munsch, Robert. "Whatever You Make of It." *Canadian Children's Literature*, no. 43, 1986.

Mutton, Wayne. "The Story Teller: Robert Munsch." *Voyager*, Fall/Winter 1989.

Nuwer, Hank. "The Vision of Maurice Sendak." *Country Gentleman*, Winter 1981.

Pasacreta, Karen. "Emily Arnold McCully: Rites of Passage." *Teaching PreK–8*, May 1998.

"Patricia Reilly Giff." The Trumpet Club Authors on Tape, Bantam, 1992.

"Peter Spier." The Trumpet Club Authors on Tape, Bantam, 1989.

Prelutsky, Jack. "Jack Prelutsky's Poetry Pages: Eloise Greenfield." *Instructor*, February 1993.

Raymond, Allen. "Faith Ringgold: 'It's Like Being a Kid All Over Again!'" *Teaching K–8*, March 1993.

———. "Tomie dePaola." *Early Years*, May 1983.

Roback, Diane. "Arnold Lobel Remembered." *Publishers Weekly*, January 29, 1988.

"Ruth Heller." A Scholastic Author Tape, Scholastic, 1992.

Sadler, Glenn Edward. "Maurice Sendak and Dr. Seuss: A Conversation." *Horn Book*, September/October 1989.

"Scholastic Salutes Donald Crews." Scholastic Book Club, n.d.

"Scholastic Salutes Illustrator Jerry Pinkney." Scholastic Book Club, n.d.

"Scholastic Salutes Joanna Cole and Bruce Degen." Scholastic Book Club, n.d.

"Scholastic Salutes Steven Kellogg." Scholastic Book Club, n.d.

"Scholatic Salutes Trina Schart Hyman." *Scholastic Book Club*, n.d.

Scieszka, Jon. "Interview Transcript." *Scholastic.com*, n.d.

Sheff, David. "Seuss on Wry." *Parenting*, February 1987.

Sis, Peter. "The Artist at Work." *Horn Book*, November/December 1992.

Slesin, Suzanne. "Quilts That Warm in New Ways." *The New York Times*, December 6, 1990.

Smith, Amanda. "Jon Scieszka and Lane Smith." *Publishers Weekly*, July 26, 1991.

Smith, A., and Diane Roback. "The Lively Art of Leo Lionni." *Publishers Weekly*, April 5, 1991.

Smith, Lane. "The Artist at Work." *Horn Book*, January/February 1993.

Steig, William. "Caldecott Award Acceptance." *Horn Book*, August 1970.

Steptoe, John. "Mufaro's Beautiful Daughters." *Horn Book*, January-February 1988.

"Steven Kellogg." The Trumpet Club Authors on Tape, Bantam, 1989.

"Steven Kellogg . . . Teachers' Co-Conspirator." *Early Years*, January 1986.

"Stevie: Realism Is a Book About Black Children." *Life*, August 29, 1969.

Swinger, Alice K. "Profile: Ashley Bryan." *Language Arts*, March 1984.

Van Allsburg, Chris. "Caldecott Medal Acceptance." *Horn Book*, August 1982.

———. "Caldecott Medal Acceptance." *Horn Book*, August 1986.

Vanderhoff, Ann. "The Weird and the Wonderful Whimsy of Robert Munsch." *Quill & Quire*, May 1982.

Van Gelder, Lawrence. "William Steig Shapes His Doodles into Prize-Winning Children's Books." *The New York Times*, November 18, 1977.

Villiani, John. "Navajo Painter Shonto Begay Talks About Two Diverse Worlds." *The New Mexican*, September 13, 1991.

Ward, Diane. "Cynthia Rylant." *Horn Book*, July/August 1993.

Watkins, Mel. "Stevie." *The New York Times Book Review*, October 5, 1969.

Wells, Rosemary. "The Artist at Work: The Writer at Work." *Horn Book*, March/April 1987.

———. "Shy Charles." *Horn Book*, January/February 1990.

———. "Words & Pictures: The Right Order." *Publishers Weekly*, February 27, 1987.

White, David E. "A Conversation with Maurice Sendak." *Horn Book*, April 1980.

Wilder, Rob. "Catching Up with Dr. Seuss." *Parents*, June 1979.

Williams, Vera. "Boston Globe-Horn Book Acceptance." *Horn Book*, February 1984.

Yolen, Jane. "Being Prepared for Serendipity." *The Writer*, May 1986.

———. "The Once-a-Year File." *The Writer*, May 1984.

———. "On Reading a Rejection Letter." *The Writer*, January 1981.

Zvirin, Stephanie, "The Booklist Interview: Jon Scieszka and Lane Smith." *Booklist*, September 1, 1992.

About the Author

JAMES PRELLER is the author of the popular Jigsaw Jones mystery series, as well as many other books for children, including *Wake Me in Spring* and *Hiccups for Elephant* (published by Scholastic). His other titles include *McGwire & Sosa: A Season to Remember* (Simon & Schuster), and *Cardinal & Sunflower* (HarperCollins). James lives in Glenmont, New York, with his wife Lisa, and three children, Nicholas, Gavin, and Maggie.